# PICTURE FRAMING

## A PRACTICAL GUIDE TO ALL ASPECTS OF THE ART AND THE CRAFT

PETE BINGHAM

with guest writers

Frances Binnington
Bernard Latter
Don Pierce

STACKPOLE
BOOKS

Published by
Stackpole Books
Cameron and Kelker Streets
P.O. Box 1831
Harrisburg, PA 17105

First American Edition 1993
Published by arrangement with Weldon Russell Pty Ltd,
107 Union Street
North Sydney, NSW 2060, Australia

Designed by: Patrick Knowles
Edited by: Kit Coppard
Special photography: Chris Gilbert; Linear Photographic; RLP Ltd
Cover photograph: Mark Gatehouse
Cover illustration: Jane Reynolds
Illustrations: Richard Draper
Picture research: Jane Lewis; Shona Wood

Typeset by Fakenham Photosetting Limited
Production by Mandarin Offset, Hong Kong
Printed in Hong Kong

10 9 8 7 6 5 4 3 2 1

Library of Congress Cataloging-in-Publication Data

Bingham, Pete
    Picture framing: a practical guide to all aspects of the art and the
craft/Pete Bingham; with guest writers, Frances Binnington,
Bernard Latter, Don Pierce. — 1st American ed.

    p. cm.

    Includes index.

    ISBN 0-8117-1175-7

    1. Picture frames and framing. I. Title

N8550.B46 1993
749'.7—dc20                                    92-36170
                                                    CIP

# CONTENTS

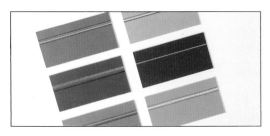

# INTRODUCTION

Since my first involvement in picture framing, back in the early sixties, there have been a number of major additions to the tools and equipment available to the framer, there is now a wealth of different materials, and there have been important advances in the field of conservation. However, nothing has changed in the basic aims of the framer – to provide the optimum setting for the art – nor has the general character of other framers altered over the years, which I have always found to be consistently cheerful.

I have intended from the outset that the book should have as much attraction and practical value to the hobby framer working in the garden shed as to the gallery owner. Thus, techniques are described both for those using simple hand tools and for those with access to commercial machinery.

The word "art" appears on the cover of this book with good reason: there is as much art in selecting and preparing the correct molding and mat or mount for a particular job, as there is in the subjects that the frame will contain. A wide variety of ideas for mat (mount) cutting and decoration, as well as for hand finishing of frames is given in the book, supported by step-by-step photographs of all the important stages, and many examples of possible effects.

There are three areas of this fascinating subject for which I have called on guest writers, each a specialist in his or her particular field: conservation and restoration; the production of manufactured moldings, and the hand finishing of frames.

The first of these is a subject of prime importance to the framer. Don Pierce is widely known and respected for his great experience in this subject. Indeed, during his term of office as President of the Professional Picture Framers' Association in America, he was responsible for establishing the first standards for the framing of art on paper. He has been involved in framing, conservation and restoration for over thirty years. An avid inventor of various pieces of equipment and products for the industry, his knowledge is far-reaching. His main concern has been to point out what can cause damage to a framed image, whether it is on canvas or on paper, so that good practice is established right from the start of its life.

Bernard Latter's knowledge of the production of moldings is extensive and thorough. This is an area in which he has worked for many years. Widely liked and respected, he is generally accepted as one of the leading experts on the subject.

Frances Binnington trained originally as a book illustrator, then became involved in hand finished moldings some twelve years ago through her husband's antique business. She became fascinated with the delicate and skilful techniques of gold leafing, and now runs regular courses on gilding in England and America.

The book, then, aims to present all aspects of picture framing from the cutting of the pieces, through hanging the frame in the home, to the conserving of the image. There are numerous ideas and examples for different decorative techniques, but as I have stated within the book, the extent of the possibilities is as wide as your imagination.

Pete Bingham

# THE
# WORKSHOP

# MITERING MACHINE:

## The Alternatives

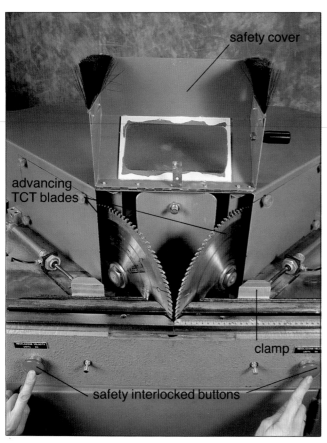

*A double miter saw with guard lifted to show blades.*

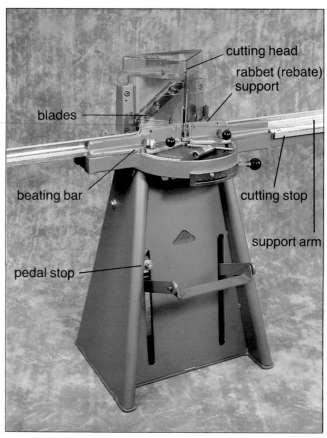

*A guillotine fitted with safety guard.*

The first half of this chapter introduces the main pieces of equipment which a picture framer who is planning to start up a workshop will need to consider. It discusses the different types of machine which perform the same function and reviews their suitability for the various kinds of framing operations.

The most important item of basic equipment for framers who cut their own moldings is the mitering machine. For the serious hobbyist or the professional there are only two types of suitable machine: electric saw or guillotine.

A guillotine or "chopper" is generally slower in operation than a saw; it requires more effort to operate, and over a long period may become quite tiring. It is also far less portable than some saws. On average, a chopper is likely to cost more than a saw of comparable quality. Against these drawbacks, however, the chopper boasts a number of important advantages.

The chopper is quieter than an electric saw. It is also cleaner: with a saw the dust flies everywhere, getting under glass and on mats (mounts). It is more accurate, more robust, has very few moving parts to go wrong, and lasts much longer than an electric saw. Adjustments are far simpler on a chopper than on an electric saw. The causes of faults are also usually more obvious – whereas problems with saws are difficult to cure unless you happen to be a wizard at electrical circuitry.

## Safety First

All machines designed to cut things are potentially dangerous. A saw is dangerous only when its blade is spinning, and you can avoid switching it on accidentally simply by removing the plug from the electrical supply. A chopper is always dangerous: the blades, hollow-ground and razor-sharp, are exposed and liable to cut the unwary finger. New machines are fitted with plastic safety guards, and they are easy to fix to existing machines. Probably the most effective safety precaution with a chopper is to make sure that the blade is never set higher than necessary. For instance, if most of the moldings you use are 1½ in (38 mm) high or less, set the pedal stop so that the blades cannot return to a position of more than 2 in (50 mm). Always leave the blades on the chopper at their furthest-in (or last-cut) position when not in use (*see photograph below*).

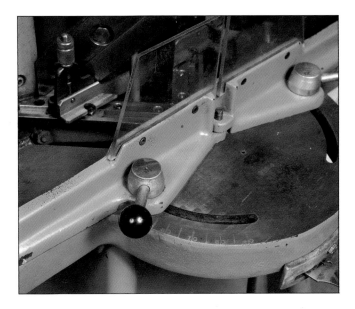

## Setting Accuracy

Another important difference between a saw and a chopper is in the accuracy of their settings for a 45° cut. Most of the cheaper saws are pre-set, so that the swiveling head of the saw locks into an appropriate angle slot. This is not always as accurate as it should be. Unfortunately, even if the discrepancy is small, it will be compounded by a factor of eight if you are assembling a four-sided frame, and even very small gaps will be glaringly obvious if the frame is made from a flat, unpatterned molding. Some double-miter saws –

machines with two identical blades, mounted at 90° to each other and driven by independent motors – can be adjusted to remove any small discrepancy.

Ideally, however, it is best to avoid the need for any adjustment. The chopper, because it is largely constructed from cast and machined metal, has fine tolerances built into the chassis of the machine, so its settings are, and remain, extremely accurate. Adjustments, where necessary, are limited to movement of the left-hand "beating" bar or vertical support against which the molding is held when cutting (*see photograph above*). Movement of this allows for the peculiarities of certain moldings to be accommodated. Say, for instance, that you have been cutting a ½ in (13 mm) wide molding. You then start to cut a 3 in (75 mm) wide one, but discover that the insides of the miters do not meet on the finished frame. You can cure this by moving the "beating" bar or support slightly away from the blades and toward you. This has the effect of presenting less wood to the blades, so reducing the offending gap. If the gap is at the back of the miter, the adjustment is made in the opposite direction, toward the blades. If, however, a gap is forming at the bottom or base of the miters, it means that the rabbet (rebate) supports are set too high, allowing more timber to be removed from the bottom of the molding section than from the top, and thus forming a gap at the base. If the gap is at the top of the miter, the supports need to be raised.

Surprisingly, gauges for setting the length of the cut required on both types of machine need to be checked for accuracy.

A saw's main advantage shows up when cutting wide moldings and those with heavily compositioned decoration. When cutting a wide molding on a chopper, you have to take several "bites," depending on the width of the molding. As a rough rule of thumb, one "bite" per ¼ in (6 mm) of molding is about average, but it will vary depending on the hardness of the timber (*see page 68*). When using a saw, because it is power-operated, no such consideration is required: the molding is cut through with one stroke of the blade. Bear in mind, however, that all electrical saws apart from the double-miter type require two cuts to form a complete corner.

An electric saw is also likely to be more effective on a molding with a heavy, plaster-molded decoration on the surface. Whereas a chopper may have a tendency to crush the decoration, the saw cuts cleanly through it. However, such heavily molded decoration is rarely used for frames nowadays, so this drawback of the chopper is more apparent than real.

### Blade Sharpening

Both types of machine require their blades to be sharpened; the interval between sharpenings is about the same for each. A good-quality saw will almost certainly be equipped with a tungsten carbide-tipped (TCT) blade. If it is not, change to a

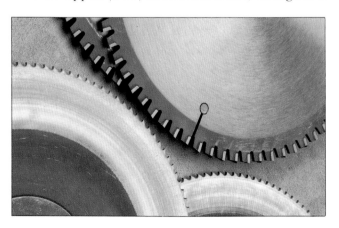

TCT immediately – its efficiency and useful life are far greater than those of normal hardened steel. TCT blades also have the advantage that if one of the "tips" comes off for any reason, another can easily be brazed on in its place. Most "saw doctors" offer this service.

Chopper blades are edged with a heated and hardened special steel, but this is in place for the life of the blade and generally cannot be replaced. As the cutting edge of a chopped blade is hollow-ground, the edge is sharpened by grinding with a

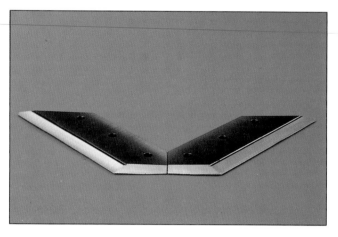

slightly concave surface. This concavity gives great advantages in ease of cut and shedding of cut material. So make sure, when having your chopper blades re-sharpened, that the operator is competent in this particular type of grinding.

Costs for sharpening saw and chopper blades are moderate, those for saw blades being slightly more expensive. Always make sure that the operator knows what is required. Do not take it for granted that he knows which edges of the chopper blades require attention.

Periods between sharpening vary with the amount of work. On average a professional framer's blades need sharpening every two months. The time is similar for saw blades, but they may last longer between sharpenings and still produce good results. Do not use worn saw blades to cut extruded aluminum molding. This takes a heavier toll on a blade than timber moldings and calls for a good, sharp saw. Aluminum cannot be cut on a chopper; but ready-mitered aluminum moldings are widely available.

Electrical saws need little routine maintenance apart from occasional lubrication of visible bearings. But make a point of removing any dust when you finish using it at the end of the day.

All the moving parts of choppers, especially those parts making metal-to-metal contact, should be lubricated with a light oil about once a week. Pay particular attention to the rabbet (rebate)-support guideways and the vertical and horizontal cutting-head guides.

### Changing Cutter Blades

Cleanliness is vitally important when changing chopper blades. When removing worn blades, ensure that they have not left any dirt behind them on the machine. Likewise, when fitting newly sharpened blades, check that the back of each blade is free of grit, then apply to it a thin coat of oil with a rag.

Work precisely and deliberately: remember, these things are razor-sharp. Blades are held in place by three large set-screws or by bolts.

A good blade-changing routine is as follows. First, remove the rabbet (rebate) supports as they will only get in the way (*see top photograph*). Clean and oil them. Then slacken all the bolts by about half a turn, using the box wrench and bar supplied with the machine (*see middle photograph*). Slight movement can now be felt in the two blades. Remove the bolts with the right hand while holding the blade in position with the left, as follows. First remove the center bolt completely on each side. This provides a hole for the thumb to hold the blade in place while the other two bolts are removed (*see bottom photograph*), and so removes the risk of the blade swinging to one side or the other and damaging itself or injuring you. Now set the bolts to one side, lift the blade free of its mounting, and lay it face down on a convenient clean flat surface. Repeat the process with the other blade. Incidentally, once the bolts have been loosened by half a turn, use the wrench by holding it in one hand and dispensing with the bar.

Changing the blade of a circular saw is simple and straightforward, usually consisting only of taking off the guard and loosening a central nut or location washer. Whether you use a chopper or a circular saw, you should have at least one spare set of blades to use while the others are away.

It is possible that you will need to work on the operating/adjusting rod, which connects the foot pedal to the chopper's cutting head – for instance, to adjust the height of the cutting head. ***Do not remove the operating bar completely from underneath the cutting head.*** The bar is the only thing that holds the cutting head up. If the bar is removed, the heavy cutting head, with blades attached, will be free to fall like a guillotine and could cause serious injury.

# UNDERPINNERS

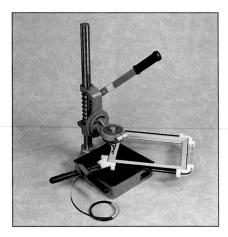

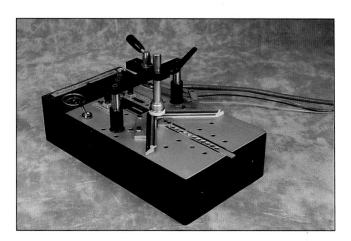

*Top: A basic, hand-operated underpinner.*
*Center: A robust, foot-operated machine.*
*Bottom: A compressed air-driven underpinner with pressure sensing clamps.*

*U*ntil a few years ago, the only specialized piece of equipment available to the framer, apart from the mitering guillotine or saw, was a miter vise. Over the years miter vises have become more and more sophisticated, evolving from simple versions for use at home to the massive foot-operated, free-standing clamps for the professional. Their sole purpose was to clamp moldings in place while a pin was inserted in the corners, to be followed by the inevitable filling-in of nail holes. Nailing was traditionally done by use of a hammer and pin and nail punch.

As technology developed, equipment such as the nail-driver was introduced. It is simply a two-part punch consisting of a nail-holder tube, at one end of which is a driver. You insert a pin head first in the tube, place the end with the point of the pin in it at the appropriate place in the corner of the molding, and strike it smartly with a hammer, so that the pin is driven home with one blow.

An important advance came with the development of the side pinner. This device was basically a pneumatic miter vise equipped with two nail guns arranged to fire pins of variable length into the traditional position on the corners of frames. Never completely effective, and often plagued by mechanical problems, the side pinner was nonetheless the first fully automatic frame-fastening system.

The underpinner appeared in France in the late 1970s, and it revolutionized the framing business. In essence it is a manually or pneumatically powered machine that inserts a wedge – a V-shaped piece of metal – into the bottom of the miter at each corner of the frame (*see page 103*).

On the simpler models, a magazine containing a block of wedges is positioned under a corner-locating device on the baseplate of the machine. When the mechanism is operated, a clamp is lowered to hold the mitered corner of the frame in a position while, simultaneously, a driver strips a single wedge from the magazine and drives it upward into the underside of the corner. Both movements are initiated by a single operation of the manual or pneumatic foot pedal.

More sophisticated designs include an automatic rabbet (rebate) clamp in addition to the main overhead clamp. And recent developments include pressure-sensing clamps, variable pressure for pneumatic models, tilting corner-locators to compensate for poorly cut moldings, and automatic gluing.

Underpinners vary considerably in price, depending on their complexity. For the professional framer producing large quantities of frames on contract, the most sophisticated models are no doubt a good investment. For the framer engaged mainly in individually commissioned work and for the keen hobbyist, the more basic models may suffice. But bear in mind that underpinning with manually operated models gets tiring after a time, especially if the moldings are made from hard timber. Almost every professional framer who starts off with a manual machine converts to compressed-air operation eventually.

### BUYING AN UNDERPINNER: 10 TIPS

1.  If possible, buy from one of the larger suppliers: they will have a bigger selection of models in their showroom and will probably offer a better after-sales service. Choose a well-known brand that has been around for long enough to establish a reputation for quality and reliability.

2.  Think twice before buying a free-standing machine. Space is at a premium in most framers' workshops, and the ideal place for the underpinner is in the corner of the framing bench (*see page 22*). Models suitable for this space are usually less expensive than the free-standing ones.

3.  If you are buying an air-powered machine, make sure it has a quiet compressor, particularly if you are a professional and your workshop is next to your gallery. Don't take the salesman's word for it that it's quiet – insist on listening to it running; some people's idea of quiet may differ from yours. In any case, there are many almost silent compressors on the market today.

4.  Look for large air-reservoir capacity: the bigger the tank, the less often the compressor will switch on and off. A small-capacity compressor will be running almost continuously when the underpinner is on an extended production run.

5.  If you are going to use the machine for long production runs, make sure that the wedge magazine is of large capacity and the cartridges are easy to install and remove.

6.  If the manufacturer recommends a certain type of wedge, make sure that you use it – and that supplies are readily available.

7.  If much of your work is with highly decorated frames, make sure that the machine's top clamp is lined with padding that will not damage the more delicate moldings.

8.  Make sure that it is easy to fit replaceable components of the underpinner – particularly the wedge driver, which is the part most likely to fail.

9.  Does the machine come with a set of tools and main spares, such as the wedge driver? If not, how much do they cost?

10. Insist that the machine you select is installed by the supplier and that you are given full instruction on its operation at your workshop.

# MAT (MOUNT) CUTTERS

*M*ost framers require only two types of mat (mount) cutter: oval and straight. Both types should cut a bevel of approximately 45°; some models will also make a vertical 90° cut.

Although cutting speed will be a factor in your choice of model, overwhelmingly its most important attribute must be its ability to make cuts of near-perfect quality. There are a lot of extremely sophisticated (and expensive) cutters on the market nowadays, but their essential job remains the same as it has always been: to cut a circular, oval, square, or rectangular opening in a piece of mat (mount) board. This obviously requires a pretty sharp blade, and razor-type blades are the usual choice; the type with a hollow-ground edge is the best. Recent additions to the array of mat (mount) cutters on the market seem to favor the craft knife type of blade, which is somewhat thicker and therefore stronger than the old single-edge razor blade. The older blades have the advantage that, being thinner, they afford a better chance of correcting small overcuts; they are also cheaper.

## ——— STRAIGHT CUTTERS ———

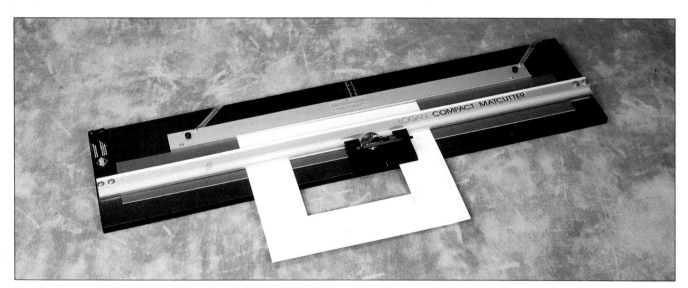

The primary function of a straight mat (mount) cutter is to make a beveled cut in a piece of mat (mount) board of six-sheet, or approximately ⅛ in (3 mm), thickness. Most mat (mount) cutters do this by cutting through from the back of the board. This is desirable for two reasons. First, it facilitates any marking out that may be required, allowing the face of the board to remain clean and free from finger-marks or other dirt. Second, and more importantly, it allows most of the board to be held down by the cutting bar of the machine. If the cut was done from the face, the machine would have to be drastically redesigned, for reasons explained in the chapter on mat (mount) cutting.

Mat (mount) cutters vary in size, but they must be large enough to make a clean cut in the longest side of a double imperial sheet of mat (mount) board – that is, about 40 in (1000 mm). The larger machines can make useful cuts of 60 in (1525 mm) and more.

A typical mat (mount) cutter has two main components: the baseboard and the cutter bar,

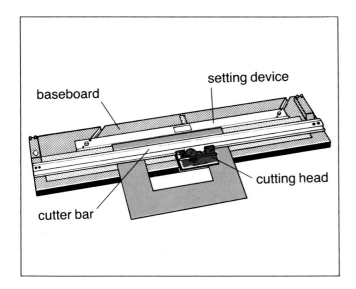

which carries the cutting head. The two are hinged together by various means. Most modern cutters have eliminated the need for lubrication by use of nylon and plastic bushings. The newer models have various setting devices and are calibrated in metric measure, though some also have imperial measure.

## OVAL CUTTERS

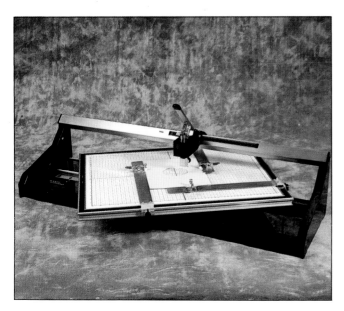

Unlike straight cutters, these cut from the surface of the board, so extra care needs to be taken to avoid marking or staining. The oval shape is obtained by two separate, adjustable components working with each other to produce an offset from a circular shape.

Most types of oval cutter work on similar lines to produce the desired effect. They usually have two basic settings, one to determine the width of the oval, the other to set the *difference* between the width and the height (or length). Thus, if you require an oval 5 in (125 mm) wide by 7 in (175 mm) high, the settings on the two scales would be 5 in (125 mm) for the width and 2 in (50 mm) for the difference between width and height. The

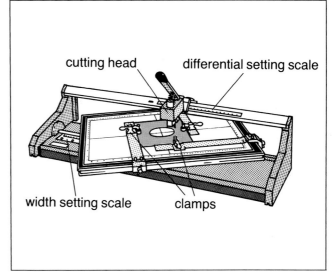

machine must have some method of holding the work in place while cutting. Most models are fitted with clips or clamps.

The work must be positioned accurately under the cutting head, so adequate means should be provided to achieve this. Perfect ovals are difficult to achieve on a machine so, when buying a new type, make certain that it will perform to a standard adequate for your needs.

There are two ways to discover any shortcomings in this respect. First, ask the salesman for a certain size oval to be cut. When this has been done, and with the board still in place in the machine, ask for the width setting to be opened out by ⅛ in (3 mm) all around. If the machine balks at this, don't buy it. Second, ask for three ovals of the same size to be cut in a row on a single piece of board. Then check that they are all at the same height from the top of the board, that they are spaced evenly, and that they are all of identical shape.

If the machine performs both these tasks

faultlessly it is probably worth buying, as long as it cuts ovals of the size you require. Probably three-quarters of all ovals cut by framers measure less than 20 × 16 in (500 × 400 mm); but this does not mean that your machine should not be able to produce larger sizes. If the salesman tells you, for instance, that 20 × 16 in is indeed the maximum oval the machine will cut, ask if this includes a margin of, say, 2 in (50 mm) all around, or is the absolute maximum with no margin allowed. This is important because if it is indeed the absolute maximum, then the practical maximum will be more like 16 × 12 in (400 × 300 mm).

The most useful machine for most framing jobs would be able to cut an oval in a full-size sheet of mat (mount) board, leaving a decent margin around the outside. Therefore, if the full sheet is, say, 40 × 32 in (1000 × 800 mm) maximum and you require a minimum 2 in (50 mm) border, the maximum practical capability of the machine should be about 36 × 28 in (900 × 700 mm).

This would require a larger machine than is generally available at present, so you have to compromise. A suitable machine will have, say, a 30 × 26 in (750 × 650 mm) top-end cut.

The mechanical geometry of these cutters means that very small ovals are difficult to achieve. But a good quality cutter should be able to produce usable ovals as small as 1½ × 1 in (38 × 25 mm).

You should also check if the machine can be easily adjusted to compensate for any mechanical idiosyncracy. For instance, some machines have a tendency, as the ovals get smaller, to cut the ovals as if they were "leaning" to one side. Make sure that this can be rectified. All pointers and scales should be capable of similar adjustments. Some machines have a restricted scale of offset (the difference between width and length of oval). A maximum offset of 4 in (100 mm) is reasonable on a 16 × 12 in (400 × 300 mm) oval, but the same offset on a 30 × 26 in (750 × 650 mm) oval makes for a rather fat shape. A 10 in (250 mm) offset would be more acceptable here. But, as always, the buyer must balance his requirements of performance and cost.

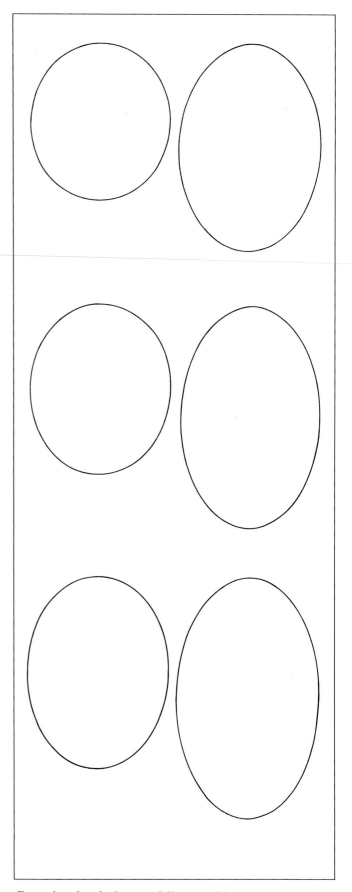

*Examples of ovals showing different width to height ratios.*

# HEAT-SEAL/ DRY-MOUNT PRESS

*H*eat-seal/dry-mount presses come in three basic forms: hard-bed, soft-bed, and vacuum. The term "bed" refers to the base area of the machine where the work is placed for processing.

The three types of press work in different ways. The soft-bed, as its name implies, has a soft cushion base, the purpose of which is to equalize pressure across the work when the top or platen is lowered. These machines use a cantilever system to operate the closing action.

The advantage of this design is that it usually allows a large format for a relatively light weight. Its main disadvantage is that it has limitations on the range of materials that can be processed. For instance, canvas bonding, a method of putting a photograph or print onto canvas, requires greater pressure than most soft-bed presses can provide. On the other hand, a soft-bed is much faster in operation than most hard-bed presses (apart from the large hydraulically powered machines).

Vacuum presses are the easiest to operate – the other two types call for more physical effort – and there are no pressures to judge, no finicky adjustments to be made, no laborious turning of wheels. Vacuum presses are particularly useful for mounting on delicate surfaces such as the light but rigid foam-cored board that has become so popular with framers. They also deal without difficulty with varying thicknesses of mat (mount); for example, $5/16$ and $1/16$ in (8 and 1.5 mm) thicknesses at the same time are nothing out of the ordinary.

**Left:** *A heavy duty hard-bed press made from steel and cast aluminum.*
**Right:** *A large format vacuum press with a transparent top panel. Both machines are suitable for dry-mounting, heat-sealing and canvas bonding.*

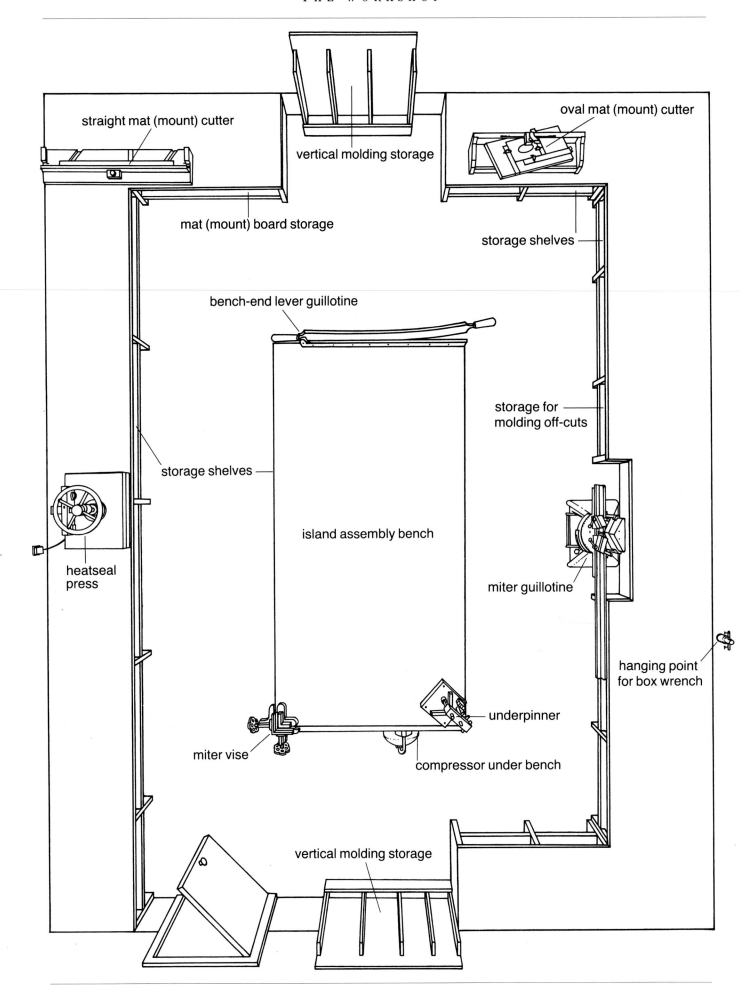

straight mat (mount) cutter

oval mat (mount) cutter

vertical molding storage

mat (mount) board storage

storage shelves

bench-end lever guillotine

storage for
molding off-cuts

storage shelves

heatseal
press

miter guillotine

hanging point
for box wrench

underpinner

miter vise

compressor under bench

vertical molding storage

island assembly bench

# LAYOUT AND FURNITURE

*F*or most framers, the perfect workshop layout is just a pipe-dream; they rarely have the time or opportunity to lay the working area out in the most logical and effective way. However, assuming that you had the space, time, and money to do the thing properly, how would you go about it?

### THE ASSEMBLY BENCH

Let us start with the assembly bench, where the frames are put together. Ideally, this should be an "island" bench which you can walk around without obstruction, so it will be located in the center of your floor area. If you are making it yourself, the design should enable you to use stock sizes of sheet materials such as chipboard, hardboard, and plywood. A surface of 8 × 4 ft (2.4 × 1.2 m) or 6 × 3 ft (1.8 × 0.9 m) is typical – the bigger the better.

The height of a workbench is a vital consideration, and depends in large measure on the height of the individual. To find the correct working height, use the following method. Bend forward so that your upper body is parallel to the floor and measure the distance from your chest to the floor. You will find that for most people the measurement will fall somewhere between 2 ft 9 in and 3 ft 3 in (0.8 and 1 m). This may seem to be a touch on the high side, but it proves to be very comfortable in practice.

Construction should be stout and solid, making sure that the top is well supported where necessary. If possible make the top with a shallow recess that will be completely filled by a 2.4 × 1.2 m (8 × 4 ft) sheet of hardboard. This gives the advantage of a permanently renewable working surface: when the hardboard becomes dirty or scratched, you simply replace it with another sheet.

*Estimating a comfortable working height for the assembly bench.*

Pay particular attention to shelving underneath the bench top. You can never have too much storage space in a workshop. Drawers are also useful to keep all the bits and pieces together that might otherwise be scattered around the workshop and eventually lost. Everyday tools always clutter up the bench: because they are in frequent use, you never put them away until the end of the day. In order to get them off the worktop, screw lengths of plastic rainwater guttering to the edges of your bench just below the overhang; this provides temporary but accessible storage for tape rules, knives, etc., leaving the top clear for the work.

Fit your underpinner to one corner of the bench, with the working surface of the machine flush with the top of the bench; this allows the bench to support the picture frame during assembly. In the diagonally opposite corner, install a standard hand-tightened miter clamp for use on the occasions when you work with a molding pattern on which you cannot use the underpinner.

If your underpinner is air-powered, house the compressor underneath the assembly bench, where it is out of the way, reasonably dust-free yet accessible for servicing or adjustment. If you need compressed air elsewhere in the workshop and have to use this single compressor, pipe the air vertically up through the bench and lead it at ceiling height to the appropriate position. On the other hand, if you frequently require compressed air, it makes sense to buy a second compressor; it's always useful to have a back-up machine.

— THE MITER CUTTER BENCH —

The siting of your mitering guillotine requires careful consideration of four important factors:

1.  You need to have easy access to the back of the machine in order to clear away the waste.
2.  You will need at least 10 ft (3 m) of uninterrupted space horizontally to the left of where the chopper blades meet.
3.  The chopper should be placed as near as possible to a surface that can be used for stacking cut pieces.
4.  You must have good access to your moldings. There is no point in having the molding racks on the other side of the workshop. On the other hand, the racks will need to be able to house molding in 10 ft (3 m) lengths, so they, too, are not always easy to site (*see page 23*).

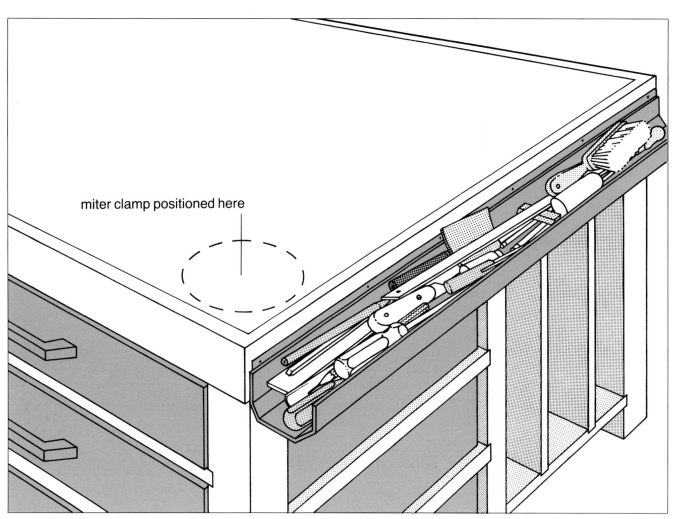

miter clamp positioned here

Make a hanging point in a prominent position for the box wrench that goes with the chopper, so that when the time comes to change the blade you know exactly where to find it. Two nails about 1¼ in (32 mm) apart and located on the front of the bench or on the wall adjacent to the machine are suitable.

Support for moldings when they are being cut is another problem. A left-hand extension arm is available as an extra with most brands of chopper; it is not expensive and you may find it useful, although it does not support a molding along its entire length. You will need some other support at least 1.8 m (6 ft) from the center of the blades. One answer to the problem is a proprietary molding support stand, which is simply a metal tripod with an adjustable bracket. An advantage of siting the machine near a bench is that you can build a hinged extension onto the edge of the bench to support the molding. It can be folded away when not in use.

## THE MAT (MOUNT) CUTTER BENCH

The straight mat (mount) cutter should be sited at the left-hand end of its own bench, and with its top level with the bench. Since all straight cutting is done from the back, the support of the bench needs to be on the right of the machine – hence the siting of the cutter on the left. The mat (mount) cutter can be fitted into a bench against the wall of the workshop as you will never need access to its far side. If you can take advantage of natural light when positioning the bench, so much the better.

The dimensions of the bench should take into account the overall size of the mat (mount) cutter, which these days averages from 40–62 in (1016 to 1575 mm) long, although many cutters are smaller. You should consider at the same time where your oval cutter will be sited. Assuming you are fitting a straight cutter which has a maximum cut of 48 in (1220 mm), the oval cutter will need to be positioned at least 50 in (1270 mm) away if it is to share the bench with the straight cutter.

The oval cutter, like the straight, is best built into the bench with its cutting surface flush with the bench top. If this is not possible – as in the case of cutters in which the table, rather than the cutting head, turns – the machine must rest on top of the bench. It makes sense to locate the cutters at opposite ends of the bench, with the straight cutter on the left, and to use the space in between for marking out, fitting, and so on.

The mat (mount) cutter bench, then, will need to be large, probably 8 × 4 ft (2.4 × 1.2m). The space beneath the worktop can be used for shelving, or it can be partitioned for storing mat (mount) board.

There are several factors to consider before deciding how to store mat (mount) board. Horizontal shelving has the advantage of supporting the board properly, and so prevents it bending. But when laid flat, the board will get dusty if stored out of its packing. Selection also becomes difficult – each color needs a separate shelf, and there is now a very extensive range of colors available. Finally, horizontal storage makes flipping through your collection of off-cuts for a suitably sized piece almost impossible.

It is better, therefore, to store your board vertically and accept the fact that the boards in some of the larger sizes will suffer bending. The problem will be lessened if your storage area is fitted with vertical divisions. These divisions will also help you to store your board in terms of different colors, sizes, and so on. Allow as much space as possible for mat (mount) board storage, or you will find that the storing of off-cuts will become a serious problem.

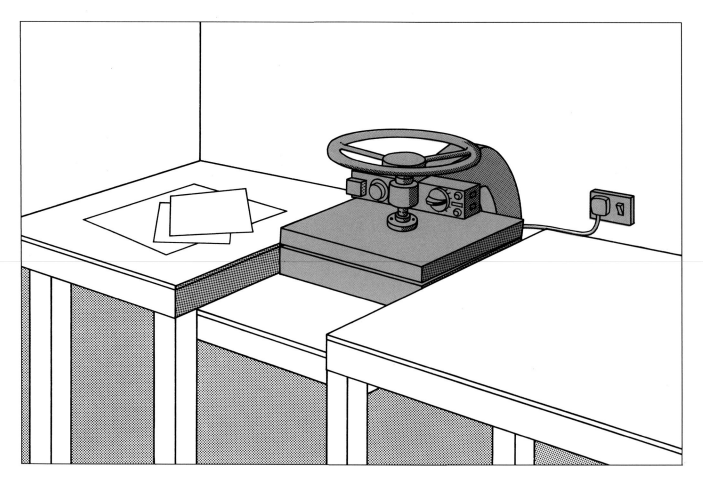

# T H E   H E A T - S E A L I N G / D R Y -
## M O U N T I N G   B E N C H

It is desirable to have a fourth bench for heat-sealing and dry-mounting operations, though it will not need to be as large as the other three. Irrespective of which type of press you choose, make a point of building it into the bench; it will repay you in speed and efficiency of work.

If you select a hard-bed press, you will need to strengthen that part of the bench structure on which the machine rests: the hard-bed types are deceptively heavy – perhaps twice the weight of equivalent soft-bed presses. The height of this bench is also important, bearing in mind that you need to exert considerable force on the lever of a soft-bed or the wheel of a hard-bed. As a rough guide, the bench top should be 4–6 in (100–150 mm) lower than those of the other three benches.

Both types of press should be positioned in the middle of the bench, with equal space on left and

right, and with the bottom plate level with the bench top. In the case of the soft-bed, this level should be established with the machine closed, locked, and set for medium pressure, otherwise you will find that in operation its cushion will be compressed lower than the surrounding bench area.

The machine should be set toward the back of the bench, the distance being governed by the platen size of the press. For instance, if you have a machine with a platen 24 in (600 mm) deep by 20 in (500 mm) wide, you can produce work with a width of up to 47 in (1194 mm) – allowing a 1 in (25 mm) overlap – by any length possible, by working in sections. The machine should therefore ideally be positioned with 24 in (600 mm) of bench top in front of it, thus allowing work to be processed with the minimum of trouble.

Again, space beneath the bench is best used for

storing the appropriate materials. It is also a good idea to devise a method of hanging your rolls of heat-seal film and dry-mounting tissue at the sides or ends of the bench. One way is to make what resemble giant toilet-paper holders.

Try to site this bench in the least-dusty area of the workshop. Heat-sealing can be ruined by dust getting stuck under the film and permanently sealed in. (It always seems to happen on your biggest, most expensive prints!)

The main items of equipment on your benches are electrically powered, so you will need to install outlets (sockets) in the vicinity of each. Outlets mounted flush with the floor may be advisable for your "island" bench. For the press bench you will need to provide an additional outlet for a tacking iron. If you are wiring the electricity in from scratch, the golden rule is that you *always* need more outlets than you think you do. You will probably find that an average of one outlet every 10 ft (3 m) of wall is about right.

## TRIMMERS

The siting of your equipment for trimming sheet materials such as mat (mount) board, hardboard and backing board must also be carefully considered. Much depends on the type of trimmer you select. The traditional type is the lever guillotine – still very widely used and possibly the most versatile and robust. Its disadvantage is that it is bulky. If it is mounted onto the end of a bench, its large guard gets in the way, and if it is the type that comes with its own table it takes up even more space. An alternative is a wall-mounted device. These are as reliable as the lever guillotine but they, too, will be unsuitable if you are short of wall space. A third type is the rotary cutter, which is more compact, but its cutting efficiency on hardboard is inferior to that of the other trimmers. The choice depends on various factors as described; however, the latest designs of wall-mounted trimmers are perhaps the best bet if you can find sufficient room on one of your workshop walls.

## STORING MOLDINGS

Molding storage is one of the most difficult problems you face when laying out a workshop. I have always found that vertical storage is best on the grounds that the moldings are more easily visible and available for selection. But this may not be possible if the workshop has a ceiling of low to average height – unless your supplier stocks moldings of shorter than average length. A simple but successful design of storage, made from melamine-faced chipboard and involving little cutting, is as follows. Basically it consists of a flat back measuring 8 ft (2.4m) square, made from two

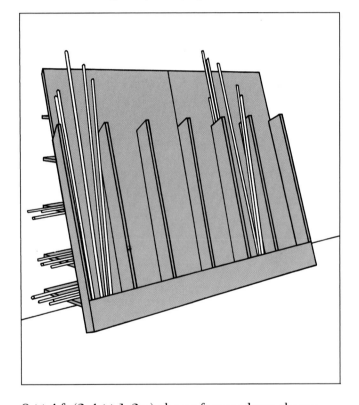

8 × 4 ft (2.4 × 1.2m) sheets fastened together; a foot at the bottom fastened at right angles to the back and measuring 12 in (0.3 m) wide by 8 ft (2.4m) long, the whole divided into compartments by use of the same 8 × 4 ft (2.4 × 1.2 m) stock pieces. The entire rack is tilted back against the wall, with the base about 20 in (500 mm) away from the wall. The space at the back can then be shelved and used for storing more moldings horizontally. The design of the basic rack module can be repeated as many times as required.

## GENERAL SHELVING

It is a good idea to put up eye-level shelving on any available wall space around the workshop, and especially in those places where you want to store items that, although not continually in use, need to be close to hand. For instance, in the mat (mount) cutting area, it is useful to have a shelf for things like glass-cleaning fluid, inks, watercolors, and other decorating equipment.

## GLASS-CUTTING

The circular saw and glass-cutting benches should both be outside the main workshop (*see page 62*). Circular saws should certainly be banned from this area: sawdust and frame assembly do not mix.

For glass-cutting, wherever it is sited, you will need a cutting bench. A good design for a glass-cutting bench is as follows. A stout top is made from ply or chipboard and mounted on well-braced legs. You will find that it is easier to work with if the top is slightly tilted toward you. An ideal slope for this is about 2 in (50 mm) over a bench depth of 4 ft (1.2 m). Suitable dimensions for the table top are 6 × 4 ft (1.8 × 1.2 m), with the front edge 32 in (810 mm) high and the back edge 34 in (860 mm) high.

This will offer a comfortable height for glass to be lifted on and off, and is easy to work at, bearing in mind that some reaching is necessary in glass cutting. The top of the bench needs to be covered with some hard-wearing but soft material. Good quality foam-backed carpet is ideal. When cutting the carpet to fit, allow a few extra inches on the depth so that it can be folded over the front edge of the bench top and fastened underneath. This will form a firm but soft cushion on the bench edge against which the glass can be leaned when maneuvering it into place.

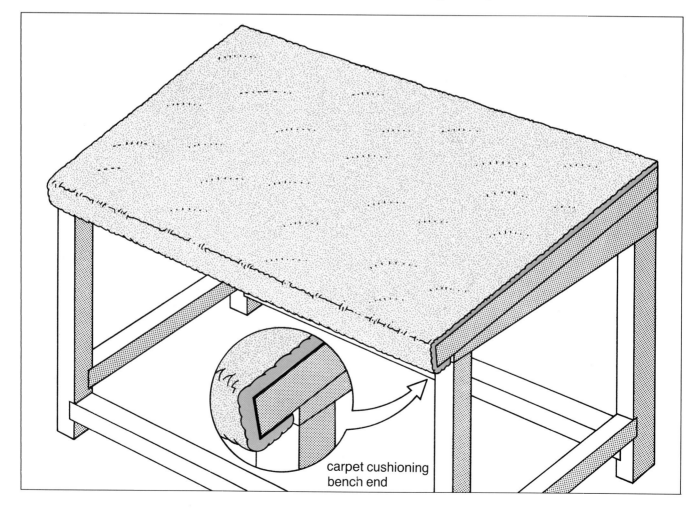

carpet cushioning
bench end

# BASIC EQUIPMENT

*A* miter can be cut with two pieces of equipment: a tenon saw and miter block or a tenon saw and miter vise. When choosing the equipment, the following tips may be useful.

First and most important, make sure that the saw is sharp. The best type to use is a saw with a heavy brass top to the tenon blade as this adds useful weight to the cutting stroke. A double miter block will give a more accurate result than the single-edged type. The metal versions with plastic guides for the angles are even better. Secure the miter block firmly to a bench; this helps immeasurably in ensuring accuracy. If cutting thick timber or a

wide, deep molding, try rubbing the saw blade with a candle – it's surprising how much easier the stroke is with this extra lubrication.

A miter vise is a useful piece of equipment, as it can double up as a corner clamp for use when assembling a frame, as described in chapter five. The simple, hand-operated underpinner is also useful for frame assembly. It is used in conjunction with a band clamp to hold the four pieces of molding in position, as shown in the photograph on page 14. Band clamps with corner blocks that slide on a metal banding are simple to use and will produce a rigid assembly.

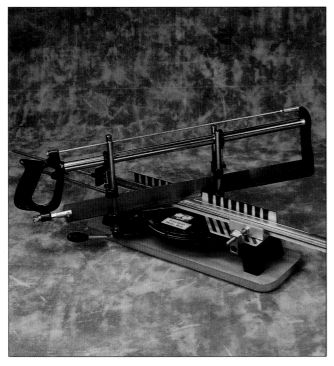 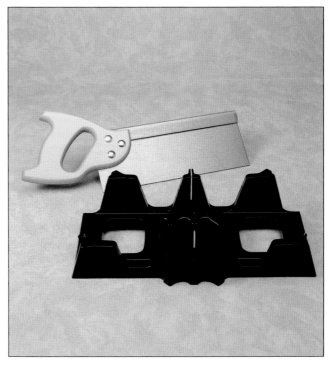

*Left: A miter block with a range of pre-set angles and an integral saw. Right: A rigid plastic miter box for use with a tenon saw.*

# SMALL ANCILLARY EQUIPMENT

*T*he following is a list of the smaller items of equipment used in the workshop, with brief descriptions of their purpose.

1 glazing gun
2 flexible point gun
3 stretching pliers
4 right-angle set square
5 craft knife
6 trimming knife
7 adhesive transfer gun
8 bradawl
9 pin hammer
10 nail punch
11 ruling pen
12 corner marking device

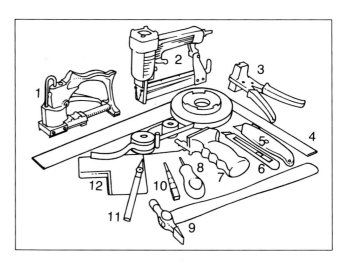

**Glazing gun**
Fastens contents of frame in place. Fires diamond or triangular darts into rebate of frame.

**Flexible-point gun**
Fires flexible points into rebate of frame. Useful if removable back is required.

**Adhesive transfer gun (ATG)**
Dispenses double-sided tape; particularly useful in mat (mount) cutting.

**Metal tape rule**
For general measuring.

**General-purpose flat rule**
For general laying out in mat (mount) cutting. Ideal length is 455 mm (18 in).

**Large right-angle set-square**
For checking square edges; used in layout in mat (mount) cutting.

**T square**
For use in marking out cuts at right angles. Some have cutouts for the glass cutter.

**36 in (915 mm) joiner's square**
For larger squaring jobs.

**Mechanical pencil**
Propelling pencil in varying hardness and thicknesses of lead. 0.5 mm HB is best for general workshop use.

**General-purpose trimming knife**
For general cutting and trimming duties.

**Craft knife**
A slimmer, finer version of above, useful for finer trimming and cutting.

**10 in (250 mm) file**
Removes burr from cut corners of aluminum moldings. Ideal version usually described in catalogs as "10-inch second cut."

**Junior hacksaw**
Useful for dismantling old frames and for general metal-cutting.

**Electrician's pliers**
For general gripping work; the insulated handles make for more comfortable use.

**Joiner's pincers**
For removing nails, pins, etc.

**Tack lifter**
Forked tool for removing largehead tacks from stretchers, etc.

**Stretching pliers**
For use when stretching canvases and tapestries.

**Glass edging pliers**
Specially shaped to remove uneven pieces of glass after a cut. Grip the offending piece and gently pull it off. Do not break downwards.

**Tacking gun**
Fires wire staples. Used in stretching pieces of needlework; heavier-duty version available for stapling canvases.

**Pin hammer**
Light hammer for use on pins up to 1¼ in (32 mm) in length.

**¾ lb (340 g) cross-peen hammer**
Nicely balanced hammer for use on pins longer than 1¼ in (32 mm).

**Bradawl**
Pointed tool for making pilot holes for screws, screw eyes, etc.

**¼ in (6 mm) blade ratchet screwdriver**
For rapid fixing of screws in general use.

**⅛ in (3 mm) blade, long-shafted screwdriver**
Provides good leverage for small screws.

**Electrician's screwdriver**
Handy tool for extra-fine screws.

**¾ in (19 mm) joiner's chisel**
Useful for scraping paper and tape from old frames prior to cleaning.

**Kitchen spatula**
Medium size is useful for separating old mats (mounts) from work prior to remounting.

**Ruling pen**
For use in wash-line mats (mounts) and ink-lining. Best types have separating nibs for ease of cleaning.

**Corner-marking device**
For wash-line decoration. Available commercially or you can make your own. To make your own, you need a small plastic 45° set-square and a 6 in (150 mm) plastic ruler. File a 45° bevel on the two sides of the right angle if the edges are not already beveled, then with the bevel underneath, tape the rule to the set-square so that it bisects the right angle. The end of the ruler should be at the point of the right angle, and the width should be to the right of this line if you are right-handed and to the left if you are left-handed.

**48 in (1220 mm) straight edge, heavy duty**
Indispensable for cutting, lining, etc.

**Brushes, paint**
Selection from No. 000 for fine touching-in to 4 in (100 mm) for painting large areas.

**Brushes, dusting**
For removal of fine-particle dirt and dust prior to frame assembly.

**Scissors, heavy duty**
For general purpose cutting of cloth, canvas, etc.

**Nail punch**
For recessing pins prior to filling.

**Clay-modeling tools**
For use with nail-hole filler when filling gaps in miters, etc.

**Oil-filled glass cutter**
Most effective hand-held glass cutter. Minute quantities of thin oil stored in hollow handle are fed through to cutting wheel. Tungsten carbide wheels cut best and last longest.

# WORKSHOP CONSUMABLES

*A* selection of minor consumables in frequent use by the picture framer.

1 aerosol spray glue
2 PVA joiner's glue
3 types of masking and sealing tape
4 gilt cream
5 nail-hole corner filler
6 woodscrews
7 Z clips
8 glazing darts
9 panel pins
10 watercolors
11 felt-tipped pens

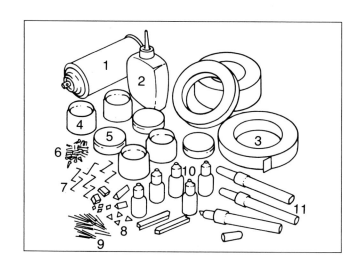

**Sealing tape**
Available in various widths; used for dust-sealing of backs.

**Masking tape**
A low-tack tape which sticks to itself for easy overlapping at corners. It can be repositioned on some surfaces.

**Water-removable tape**
For hinging conservation work to mat (mount) backs, etc.

**Double-sided tape**
Used with a proprietary dispenser. There are various types, so check which dispenser is the right one for your favorite tape.

**PVA joiner's glue**
Thick white polyvinyl acetate woodworking glue for secure jointing of miters.

**PVA builder's adhesive**
Thinner version of above, useful for general pasting jobs. Water-thinned. Its adhesive properties can be re-activated, after it has dried, by the application of heat – when it can be used as a cheap dry-mounting agent.

**Aerosol spray glue**
For those quick stick-down jobs – certificates, etc.

**Solid glue stick**
This has many uses for quick fixing; it is particularly useful for gluing back marbled paper when in strips.

**PVA paint**
Useful for coloring undermats (mounts) in double mats (mounts) and as a basecoat for gilding and re-finishing mats (mounts).

**Watercolors**
For general use in wash lining and, when diluted, as ink. Standard colors, as found in small artist's box, will suffice.

**Felt-tipped pens**
A selection is useful for restoring colors to bare, light wood at miters, etc,

**Kraft paper**
High-quality brown paper for dust-sealing picture backs.

**Display suede velvet**
Interior designer's material, often found on the walls of higher-class discos. Useful in mat (mount) decoration.

**Bookbinder's paper**
Marbled and decorated papers used in bookbinding. Effective if stuck on mats (mounts) in varying widths. Handmade versions are particularly attractive, but expensive.

**Mat (mount) cutter blades**
Always keep a good stock of blades for your machines.

**Thin machine oil**
For maintenance of various items of machinery.

**Sandpaper**
Keep various grades from coarse to fine for use on hand-finished moldings and other small smoothing jobs.

**Glass cleaner**
Modern proprietary brands are excellent, but you can make your own more cheaply by mixing denatured alcohol and water in equal parts.

**Cleaning cloths**
Must be lint-free for glass. Old dish-towels and linen bedsheets are ideal.

**Nylon cord**
In various grades for hanging your pictures.

**D-rings**
In single- and double-hole types. Fix to frame with screws.

**Screw eyes**
Also in various grades, for lighter hanging duties.

**Panel, veneer, and molding pins**
Pins of various grades for use when nailing moldings together. Veneer are the finest grade, panel pins the coarsest.

**Woodscrews**
Various gauges to suit different applications. $\frac{1}{2}$in (13 mm) No. 4 gauge "cheese" head are probably the most useful; Philips or cross-head are easier to use. Suppliers commonly pack them in 200s.

**Glazing darts**
For use in the glazing gun; either diamond or triangular in shape, $\frac{2}{5}$ in (10 mm) for general work, $\frac{1}{2}$in (13 mm) for larger jobs.

**Bifurcated rivets**
D-type split rivet used when attaching hanging devices to backs rather than to frames.

**Hinges and clips**
Used for attaching strut backs to frames for free-standing photographs, etc.

**Z-clips**
For fastening stretchers into frames; so-called because of their shape. Flexipoints and staples are quicker and more effective.

**Paper towels and dispenser**
Useful for general wiping, mopping up, etc.

**Artist's eraser**
For removing dirty thumb marks, etc, from mat (mount) board.

**Nail-hole corner fillers**
Wax-type substances, in various colors to match those of moldings, for filling corners, etc.

**Gilt cream**
For touching in gold moldings; available in various shades.

**Gilt varnish**
A range of colors applied by brush. They can be mixed for an exact color match.

**Underpinner wedges**
Ideally you should keep three sizes in stock – perhaps 7 mm, 10 mm and 12 mm.

# THE MAT
# (THE MOUNT)

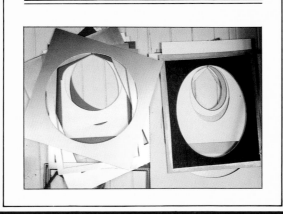

# I: MAT (MOUNT) CUTTING

*T*he original purpose of a mat (mount) was simply to keep the picture away from the glass protecting it. Beveled edges were later introduced to enhance the effect of the cut-out. The mat (mount) remained in this basic form for many years. Cutting of the board was invariably done by hand and required great skill, not to mention strength, to achieve perfect results. Cutters were usually modified versions of tools designed for some other purpose. Wood chisels, for instance, would be ground and honed to razor-sharp edges; and woodworker's files were also adapted.

Today the mechanical mat (mount) cutter is indispensable. The first such machines appeared around the turn of the century. They immediately removed one of the most laborious chores from the work of a framer and turned it into a simple and speedy operation. These early machines, though revolutionary, were pretty basic compared with the highly sophisticated types available today, and for many years were used simply to cut very basic mats (mounts).

It has been only in the past 30 years or so that mat (mount) cutting has become more adventurous. Since the introduction of highly accurate devices for setting border sizes, together with various attachments to enable fine adjustments to be made, the framer has been able to give full reign to his imagination. Almost any shape is possible to achieve – not always to the benefit of the subject being framed.

### Visual Balance

The first thing a framer must learn is an appreciation of visual balance of a mat (mount) when the frame is assembled. If it is cut with all its borders equal in width, the bottom border will appear narrower than the top. This is an optical illusion, but one that needs to be compensated for.

The obvious solution is to make the bottom border wider than the top – but by how much? Opinions vary on this subject, but the following formula will serve as a basis for your own calculations.

For finished mats (mounts) up to a size of 16 × 12 in (400 × 300 mm) the bottom borders are made ¼in (6 mm) wider than the top borders. For sizes from 16 × 12 in up to 20 × 16 in (400 × 300 mm to 500 × 400 mm), the difference will be ⅜ in (9 mm); and, for larger sizes, ½in (13 mm). There are some exceptions to this formula, but they are mostly governed by particular requirements which will be discussed later. The balance rule is not adhered to slavishly, as some mass-production requirements at the lower end of the market may dictate otherwise and equal-sided mats (mounts) are much quicker to cut than those with a balance.

## DIFFERENT TYPES OF MAT (MOUNT) BOARD

There are basically three types of mat (mount) board. All come in a wide range of colors with plain and textured surfaces, as follows:

### Standard board
This is made from a basic wood pulp, with a colored surface paper and a backing paper. Many of the boards in this range now have surface and backing papers which are "pH neutral". For standard framing. It should be mentioned, however, that there is a growing concern that the neutrality of these boards may not be permanent. The same applies to the following category.

### "Conservation quality" board
Made from chemically-treated wood pulp, this is free from lignin, alum and residual bleaching agents. For use where the requirement is for minimal contamination of art on paper.

### "Museum quality" board
This is made from 100% cotton "rag" fibre. It is completely acid free. The board is also buffered with calcium carbonate as an added protection against environmental pollution. For use in high quality work where a totally sterile environment is required for the artwork, that is, where great care is to be taken to preserve the art because it is valuable either in terms of money or for personal reasons. It has solid color throughout and therefore is the perfect medium for carved mat (mount) decoration (*see page 45*).

## CHOOSING A MAT (MOUNT) COLOR

Look for a clue in the middle of the image and err on the side of pale colors rather than dark.

Similarly, the combination of light over dark in a double mat (mount) is generally more effective than vice versa. When matching black and white images, look carefully at the darkest areas. They may, in fact, be dark brown or very dark blue and a mat (mount) in a matching color will then be much more satisfactory.

It is preferable to choose a color to match the image rather than the surroundings, but co-ordinating with the surrounding decoration could be a secondary consideration.

*A selection of mat (mount) board types. On the left side (working from top to bottom): standard quality; conservation quality; museum quality; metallic standard. On the right, in the same order: standard quality; black-core standard; mottled and textured standard. In the center: lightly-textured standard.*

# USING A HAND-HELD CUTTER

*T*here are many budget-priced, hand-held mat (mount) cutters on the market, which will produce mats (mounts) of excellent quality. The technique is simple and the equipment basic. Apart from the cutter, all you need is a good, heavy, straight edge.

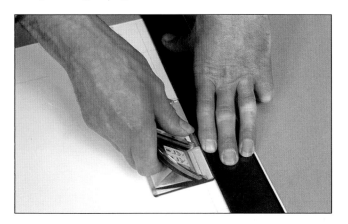

Hand cutters are best used from the back of the board as with a normal cutter. Begin by finding out the exact distance between the running edge of the cutter and the point at which the blade appears on the face of the board after cutting through it. This will help you to judge where to place the cutter at the start of a cut and where to finish. Make sure that the blade protrudes just enough to penetrate the board cleanly and no further. When cutting, concentrate on keeping the cutter flat against the board, whilst at the same time following the straight edge accurately.

Because of the difference in degrees of accuracy between a hand-held cutter and a machine, it is advisable when using the former to cut the opening in the mat (mount) first, and trim the borders to size afterwards.

# DOUBLE MATS (MOUNTS)

*A* double mat (mount), as its name suggests, consists of one superimposed on another, the idea being to allow a small edge of the lower, or undermat (mount), to show around the edge of the opening. This allows you to show a complementary or contrasting color or to promote a feeling of depth as a visual lead-in to the subject. You can produce a double mat (mount) as follows.

## General cutting equipment

mat (mount) cutter – mechanical or hand-held
metal straight edge*
flat rule
pencil
pin or similar†
masking tape
double-sided tape

\* The straight edge is for use in conjunction with a hand-held cutter.
† A sharp pointed instrument is needed to mark the mat (mount) board.

*1* Establish the overall size of the finished mat (mount) by measuring the size of opening required and adding the appropriate border widths. Cut the board to this finished size.

*2* Cut a second piece of board – the undermat (mount) – roughly ¼ in (6 mm) smaller than the mat (mount).

*3* Place the mat (mount) face down on the bench. Then stick the undermat (mount), face down, on the back of the first. You can use masking tape along two edges for this.

*4* Mark out the settings for the borders from the edge of the top mat (mount). When cutting at these settings, ensure that the blade of the cutter protrudes from its holder just enough to cut through only one thickness of board. When all four sides are cut, separate the two pieces.

*5* Mark out the setting for the top mat (mount), reducing the width of its border to correspond with the amount of border the undermat (mount) is required to show. On double mats (mounts) up to about 14 × 12 in (350 × 300 mm) in size, allow ⅛ in (3 mm) of the undermat (mount) to show; on larger mats (mounts) allow ³⁄₁₆ in (4.5 mm). The top mat (mount) can now be cut.

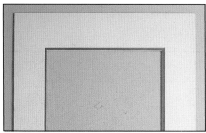

*6* Stick the two mats (mounts) together using double-sided tape, carefully aligning the top mat (mount) over the undermat (mount). The procedure can be repeated to produce triple or even quadruple mats (mounts).

**Oval cutters**
Because oval cutters work in an entirely different way, the procedure for cutting double oval mats (mounts) is also entirely different. Basically, it is just a matter of cutting two ovals that differ in size by the amount of undermat (mount) required to be shown. However, in order to allow for any slight discrepancies in the machine (and they are always there, no matter how well the machine has been set up), always start with the two pieces of board cut slightly larger than the projected finished size.

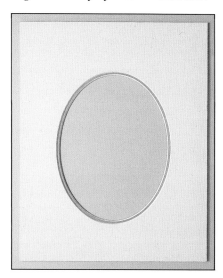

Then, when the two ovals have been successfully lined up and fixed together, trim the two together by the simple expedient of placing the glass from the frame onto the mat (mount) and marking around it.

# INLAY MATS (MOUNTS)

A similar effect to the double mat (mount) can be achieved by use of the inlay method. This is a process where two different colors can be used in a single thickness of board by cutting and laying one color inside another.

Preparation of an inlay mat (mount) starts off with the same initial steps as for a double mat (mount): you cut two pieces, one ¼in (6 mm) smaller than the other, and stick them together. Now proceed as follows:

*1* Mark out on the back of the undermat (mount) a setting equal to the finished opening size *minus the width of contrast-colored mat (mount) required*. This can now be cut, and the two pieces separated, but take care to retain the same setting on the cutter and also to keep the center cut-out.

*2* Cut the second piece of board (or the top mat (mount)) at the same setting.

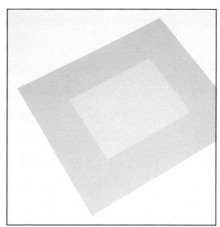

*3* Take the center cut-out from the first cut, place it in the cut-out of the top mat (mount), and tape in place.

*4* Open out the settings by the required amount and re-cut.

This cut is now the finished opening size, but is only one mat (mount) board thick – very useful if you are working with a restricted depth of rebate. Again, the process can be extended to introduce as many colors as required in one mat (mount) thickness.

An inlay panel can also be produced by the same method, slightly modified. The overall size of the finished mat (mount) is determined in the usual way, two pieces of board are cut as for the double, and secured together in the same way.

The first cuts are made using the same procedure as for the previous inlay, but the cut is made where the *outer edge* of the inlay panel is to be. One is laid inside the other and the cut is taped in place on the back as in the previous inlay. The panel width required is then set and cut. The

procedure is then repeated until the opening size is reached, leaving a panel of contrasting color laid inside another of the same thickness.

# V-GROOVING

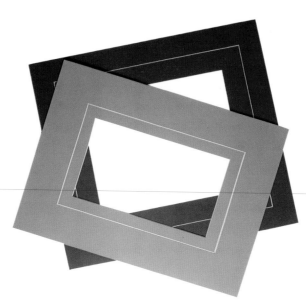

*A*nother variation on this type of cutting is what is known as V-grooving. The object is to produce a 45°-sided cut as a decorative feature around the border of the mat (mount), thus exposing the different-colored core of the board. A V-groove is produced as follows:

*1* Cut the board to its desired overall finished size, as already described.

*2* Working from the back as before, mark the settings corresponding to where the V-groove is to appear on the border.

*3* Make the cut, but while doing so make a mark with a pencil across the line of the cut, to use as a reference later.

*4* Complete the cut, retaining the center cut-out, and remove from the cutter.

*5* Take the center cut-out and return it to the cutter, placing it face up with ⅛ in (3 mm) of the edge, with the bevel underneath, showing under the cutter bar.

*6* Cut off this ⅛ in, producing a 45° cut on the surface of the board. Repeat this cut on the remaining three sides of the center cut-out.

*7* Place the cut-out face down and position the originally cut mat (mount) over it, also face down. Line them up by using the penciled reference point made in stage 3 above.

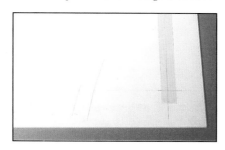

*8* Tape the center cut-out in place. Turn the mat (mount) face up and you will see the V-groove effect.

*9* Turn it face down again and cut the normal mat (mount) to its required opening size. The V-groove mat (mount) is now complete.

This procedure can be repeated to make as many V-grooves as you require. By mixing the procedure with part of the inlay method, V-grooves with different colors can be achieved.

# TITLE CUT-OUTS

*Indiamen in the China Seas*

*I*f you are framing a print that has a title on its border below the image, or if you wish to add a title, a cut-out in the mat (mount) to accommodate this can be very effective.

The first thing to check, if the title is on the print border, is that it is exactly in the middle of the paper. Then measure the size of the opening required to reveal the title, allowing a reasonable clearance around the letters. It is best to cut the opening for the title before the main opening in the mat (mount). When calculating the overall size of the mat (mount), bear in mind that the border containing the title opening will probably need to be wider than normal – although this will, of course, be governed by the size of the opening required. Now proceed as follows:

*1* Cut the board to the finished size, as described already.

*2* Mark a center line on the back, and check the position of the title on the print. If the title is relatively close to the image area, you may have to make the mat (mount) edge overlap the bottom of the image area more than normal in order to give yourself enough space to position the title opening effectively. You should allow a space of at least ¼ in (6 mm) between the bottom of the bevel on the main mat (mount) opening and the bottom of the bevel on the title opening.

*3* Mark out the width of the title opening on either side of the center line, and extend the lines marked as far as you can across the board: the longer the lines, the more accurate will be the lining up in the cutter.

*4* Mark out, first, the main mat (mount) opening, then the top of the title opening. Work from the appropriate edge of the main opening, bearing in mind the minimum-measurement rule.

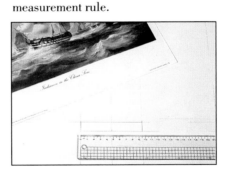

*5* Mark out the depth of the title opening, again extending the lines as far as possible.

*6* Cut the title opening, bearing in mind that each bevel cut must slope away from the middle of the board. Pay particular attention to accurate lining up of the marked lines.

*7* Cut the main opening. Cutting a title opening in a double mat (mount) is more difficult, but as long as your marking out is accurate there is no reason why you should not be successful.

More elaborate ideas for producing mats (mounts) with the straight cutter are limited only by your imagination. Most decorative mat (mount) cutting falls into one of two basic categories: fancy corners and border panel cut-outs. From a technical viewpoint, highly intricate cut-out work is the most exciting to do, but it will not necessarily produce the best final result. Fancy cut-outs can sometimes draw attention away from the subject being framed. A mat (mount) that looks like Belgian lace may be very impressive at a mat (mount) cutter demonstration – but what sort of image is going to look good inside it?

# FANCY CORNERS

$S$ ome of the most effective mats (mounts) are created by using both oval and straight cutters on the same mat (mount) to produce combinations of ovals, circles, rectangles, and squares. One simple combination is the arched top mat (mount) (1 in the drawings), which is an oval squared off at the bottom with the straight cutter. You have to be very careful when joining the straight cut to the oval (the latter is always cut first); a small "blip" usually appears where the two bevels meet. This can be removed by careful use of a small piece of very fine grade sandpaper.

The discontinuity can be avoided by making the rectangle wider than the oval and joining the two with a straight cut to form small "corners" (2). Alternatively, you can cut small circles instead of the corners (3), producing a slightly oriental effect. This particular type is best done when you have had plenty of practice with the oval cutter, as it involves some complicated laying out.

Another simple but attractive form is made by cutting an oval and then superimposing on it a wider but shorter rectangle (4). If you make the rectangle both narrower and shorter (5), you have an effective variation. Extend the length of the rectangle to that of the oval (6) and it changes the effect again.

By taking the first arch-top version and making the base wider but joining the straight sides at a tangent makes yet another change (7). Cutting double corners at the top of the oval (8) produces a domed temple effect; while (9) hints at the infinite

---

*Special-effects cutting equipment*

| | |
|---|---|
| slim craft knife | smooth embossing tool* |
| pencil | PVA paint |
| very fine sandpaper | |
| double-sided tape | * See page 46 |

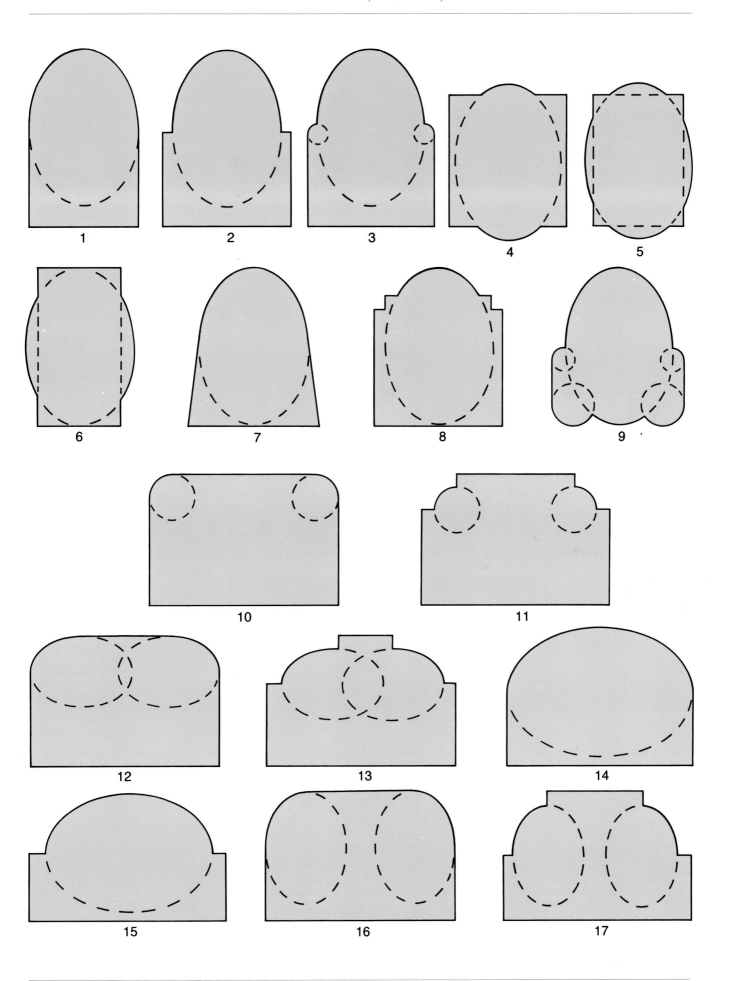

range of effects available by use of ovals, circles, and straight cuts. Although seemingly complicated, these examples should present no real problem and are certainly worth the effort.

The second set of examples reverses the procedure of the first: straight cuts, with ovals added. The first example (10) has two circles cut first at appropriate positions in the board, followed by straight cuts. Again, any small "blips" where the two bevels meet can be removed with fine sandpaper. Figure 11 is the same idea but with the position of the circles moved inward and downward, the corners then being cut and the shape being completed with the straight cutter.

The third example (12) is essentially the same idea as the first, but using ovals instead of circles. The positioning and cutting of the two ovals, however, are entirely different as the ovals have to be "stacked" above each other and "vertical" on the machine, whereas the circles may be cut side by side, or "horizontal." The sizes of the circles and ovals can be varied, but ensure that the oval or circle used to shape the corner stays within the confines of the required opening size. The next mat (mount) (13) is similar in principle to 11, but again uses ovals instead of circles.

The fifth design in this second set (14) is perhaps the simplest as it requires the minimum of the cutting and finishing; it is also one of the most useful. The next one (15) is the now familiar variation, while 16 and 17 continue the same theme but with vertical ovals.

All these examples are intended merely as a basic guide, to be expanded on. Another rectangular mat (mount) around examples 10–17, for instance, would add considerably to their appeal without making them fussy.

The variety and ingenuity of your mat (mount) designs should be limited only by your imagination and good taste. It can be very rewarding work – financially for the professional looking to attract custom by the exclusiveness of his or her designs; aesthetically for the hobbyist taking pride in his or her creative talent. But guard against use of over-complex designs and garish combinations of colors. A striking combination is a triple mat (mount) of an oval with a double rectangular mat (mount) around it, all in the same shade of 100% rag board. The subtle effects of shadow on the differently shaped bevels are enhanced by the single color of the three boards. This type of combination is particularly useful when framing old photographs.

# BORDER PANEL CUT-OUTS

You can produce fascinating effects by "carving" mat (mount) board – that is, by cutting shapes in the board with a slim craft knife. First of all, select a theme for the carved decoration and lightly sketch it in on the mat (mount) surface.

Then, working with the blade at an angle of about 45°, trace the shape with the blade, applying medium pressure. Now turn the board around completely and make a parallel cut alongside the first, close enough so that a sliver of board becomes detached and removable. It is best to select simple "flowing" shapes for this effect, such as leaves and intertwining vines. Art Nouveau shapes lend themselves very effectively to this technique, see page 61 for some examples.

Solid-color rag board is by far the best medium for these carved effects, not only because of the board's composition, but also because the board is the same color all the way through. The colored or black-cored boards also work well, but the effect with these is more startling than subtle. Try using them around an oval or in a V-groove panel, or in conjunction with just a single V-groove. Above all, use a sharp blade; one blade per mat (mount) is the ideal situation.

## SOLID RAG BOARD

It's worth taking time to consider the advantages that the physical properties of rag can give you. For instance, the edge of a mat's (mount's) cut-out does not *have* to be 45° bevel. The fact that solid rag is not a laminate of papers allows the board to be sanded. With judicious use of very fine sandpaper, a 45° bevel can be turned into a rounded edge. The bevel can also be made more shallow by sanding.

When using these techniques, it is a great advantage to make up your own sandpaper "files." These are really purpose-made nail-boards. Cut some strips of mat (mount) board about 9 × ¾ in (230 × 19 mm), and cover 6 in (150 mm) of both sides of these with the appropriate grade of sandpaper, using double-sided tape to stick them together.

Try some double mats (mounts) using 45° bevels and rounded edges together, or be more adventurous and do a triple mat (mount) with a mixture of a bevel, a rounded-edge, and a simple vertical cut, all in solid-color rag; the effects are quite stunning.

# E MBOSSING

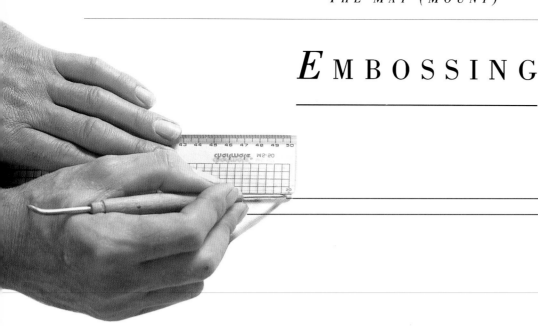

S olid rag board also lends itself very well to engraved decorations, or embossing. This is quite a simple addition to the cut mat (mount). On a straight or rectangular mat (mount), the start and finish points are marked in the same way as for an ink line (*see page 54*). The embossed line can then be applied using a smooth embossing tool of the type used by leather craftsmen. (These are widely available from craft shops and are a very useful addition to the framer's tool box.)

To add an embossed line to an oval mat (mount) is much quicker and easier. Proceed as follows:

*1* Cut the oval to the required size.

*2* Open the cutter setting for the width to the required position for the embossed line.

*3* Remove the blade cutting head and replace it with the glass-cutting wheel.

*4* Starting the embossed line on a piece of scrap board and using appropriate pressure to create the required impression, turn the oval cutter head until a satisfactory line is produced.

Because the cutter can produce accurate results, embossed lines close together can easily be achieved.

Embossing can be produced on standard mat (mount) board, but the results do not have the same subtle effects.

## WORKING WITH THICK MAT (MOUNT) BOARD

Sometimes it is desirable to produce a mat (mount) from thicker than normal board. Mount board in Britain is measured in "sheet" thickness; a thin board is called 4-sheet, standard board would be 6-sheet, and thicker board would be 8-, 10-, or even 12-sheet, although the last is now extremely rare. The term "sheet" refers to the number of layers of paper that make up the board. In the United States, there is simply single thick or double thick. Single thick (6-sheet) is by far the more commonly used type of board.

The biggest problem with the thicker boards, as may be imagined, is cutting them. Mat (mount) cutters are designed to work for most of their lives on the standard thickness. When the thicker versions come along, problems begin to appear. Because the thicker boards (double-thick) are twice the thickness of standard ones, the blade on the mat (mount) cutter has to protrude twice as far as normally, and consequently it is inclined to bend. The first manifestation of this problem is a curve on the bevel, starting at the corner.

This will occur to some degree on all mat (mount) cutters at some time. One way of eliminating it is to make the cut twice. Make the first cut with the blade set for cutting standard-thickness board. Then extend the blade so that it will fully penetrate the board, and repeat the cut. This obviously takes more time, but the results are perfect, and the blades last longer. Do not forget to start and finish the cuts an appropriate amount in advance of and past the marked points on the mat (mount) to allow for the extra thickness of the board.

Oval cutters present no such problems with thick board because of the mechanical characteristics of the machines, and they will cut 10-sheet board with no effort at all.

# FOAM-CORED BOARD

*A*nother alternative to normal thick mat (mount) board is foam-cored board, which is available in various thicknesses and in acid-free varieties. The two thinner versions of this material cut superbly well on mat (mount) cutters – and with no recourse to double-cutting. The only problem with this is that, when cut, the foam center is exposed. You can use the following procedure for producing deep bevels on double mats (mounts) using foam-cored board. First, cut the foam-core as you would cut a normal undermat (mount) on a double. This obviously eliminates the miters at the corner but leaves the unsightly core of foam. Now paint the bevel with three coats of PVA paint. The foam will

become filled in with the thick texture of the paint and will look like normal mat (mount) board but with a superb, super-deep bevel. You will get the best results by lightly sanding with fine paper between each application of paint. Again, this method is more time-consuming than normal, but the results are well worth the extra effort.

Foam-core has many other uses which are a boon to the innovative framer. One is as spacing material when a gap or depth has to be filled – for instance, when framing *découpage* (subjects which have a three-dimensional depth to them but require a mat (mount)). Foam-core is perfect for making up this depth. The ³⁄₁₆ in (4.5 mm) foam-core is exactly the same thickness as the flat gold slip that is used frequently by framers, and so is ideal for this application. It is also useful if you are mounting and framing medals. You may find that the medals are not thick enough to justify making a box mount. Say, for example, that you wish to frame three medals. What you need is three circles about ⅛ in (3 mm) deep. A problem arises if the surface the medals are to be mounted on is to be covered with a velvet material. The following is a method to get around the problem.

## Materials

foam-cored board
PVA builder's adhesive
display velvet
dry-mounting press
builder's waterproof sealant

*1* Decide on the size of circles required, add on the required surrounding border, and then select a piece of foam-core scrap somewhat bigger than this of the required ³⁄₁₆ in (4.5 mm) thickness.

*2* Cover this with the relevant material, which can be stuck on with PVA builder's adhesive.

*3* Take another scrap piece of extra-thick board, say 12-sheet or ⅛ in (3 mm) thickness, and cut from this a beveled circle of the size required to accommodate the medal in question, taking care to allow some clearance around the subject.

*4* Place the cut disk of board roughly in the middle of the fabric-covered foam-core, place under the platen of the cold dry mounting press, and close the press, applying considerable pressure.

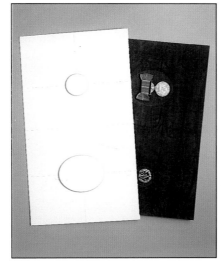

*5* Remove the disk and foam-core from the press and you will find a neat impression of the disk to the required depth in the velvet-covered foam-core.

*6* Stick the medals in place. For this the best medium is the thick, rubberoid solution that builders use for sealing roofing and rainwater guttering; but be very careful when applying it as it can be very messy.

*7* Trim the finished piece by cutting the size of glass required, placing it on the subject and marking around it.

This process can also be used with ovals, making it useful for framing objects such as cameos. If extra depth is required, simply increase the thickness of the press-die by introducing another complementary shape around the first, producing a type of double mat (mount) in reverse. Mixtures of shapes work well in this context, such as a rectangle around an oval or a square around a circle.

# USING BEVELED SLIP

*M*any framers use a lot of flat "slip" – mainly the ½in (13 mm) variety with a fluted bevel along the sight edge. When used in conjunction with a mat (mount), the effect is quite elegant, especially if the board is covered with display velvet. Try the following method:

*1* Establish the image area required and make up a slip to this size.

*2* Working about ¹⁄₁₆ in (1.5 mm) back from the top of the fluted bevel on the slip, add on the required borders of the finished mat (mount), and cut a piece of board to this size. If the velvet is to be wrapped around the bevel, the mat (mount) is cut at this point.

*3* Cut four strips of velvet of appropriate length and width, taking care to allow enough width to wrap the velvet around to the back of the board; 1 in (25 mm) extra is usually sufficient.

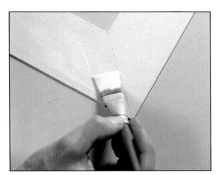

*4* Paste the top surface of one border of the mat (mount) with PVA glue, painting the glue carefully at a 45°

angle between the corners of the board and the top corner of the bevel. Cover the bevel with adhesive as well.

*5* Apply a strip of velvet, carefully aligning one edge with the outer edge of the mat (mount).

*6* Turn the board over, face down, and cut the remaining 1 in (25 mm) or so of the overhanging velvet, alongside the adjacent bevels, thus allowing the overhang to be folded over to the back.

*7* Apply adhesive to the back, pull the velvet tightly around the bevel, and press it firmly in place in the

adhesive, taking care not to allow any onto the surface.

*8* Turn the board over, face up. Place a straight edge from the corner of the board to the point at the top corner of the bevel. Trim off the excess material with a craft knife, paying particular attention to the bevel – the angle alters slightly here.

*9* Apply double-sided tape to the slip, taking care that no tape shows on the exposed edge, and position the covered mat (mount) carefully on this. Alternatively, the velvet can be applied before the mat (mount) is cut. This is obviously much easier, and the resultant white bevel edge can be quite attractive. In each case, the difference on the back of the mat (mount) between the slip and the board can be made up with ³⁄₁₆ in (4.5 mm) foam-core.

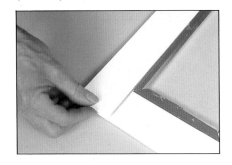

Among the myriad other materials for covering mats (mounts) is an interesting American product: a self-stick, real wood veneer which has almost endless possibilities in the field of mat (mount) cutting. It is extremely thin and can be cut, folded, and bent as necessary. It can also be stained and polished. It is particularly useful as an exterior mat (mount) or slip to complement a particular feature of a subject.

# 2: MAT (MOUNT) DECORATION

*T*here's a very fine dividing line between mat (mount) cutting and mat (mount) decoration. For many the mat (mount) is the core of picture framing. Decorating the mat (mount) provides the subtle finishing touch to the framer's craft; it can make all the difference between a design that's excitingly apt for the subject matter of the picture and one that is merely competent.

Mat (mount) decoration has been an artform of its own for as long as pictures have been framed. Even if it consists merely of a single ink line, it can still have the effect of enlivening an otherwise blank expanse of border between the subject and the frame. Indeed, the humble ink line is where most people start their mat (mount) decorating; but there are some basics you need to know even before attempting this.

### First Steps
Before drawing a line, you must know where to start and finish; and this, of course, involves marking these points on the surface of the mat (mount). The technique of marking out is made much easier with the use of a corner-marking device (*see page 29*). The first step in ink-line drawing is to obtain one of these and to become familiar with its use. The next step is to equip yourself with a suitable ruling pen. The best pens have a splittable nib for ease of cleaning; the nib-blade is wide and holds a useful amount of ink.

Watercolor inks can be attractive, but they have the disadvantage that they are not opaque, so they will not show as a light color on a dark background. The best inks are the PVA paint-derived types. They have a high surface density, are more resistant to "blobbing" and – most important of all – produce a good solid color even on the blackest of black boards.

When you have assembled all the equipment necessary for drawing ink lines, the next step is to practise using it. Draw thin lines and thick lines and practise joining lines at corners; experiment with drawing lines close together, then try merging them to produce extra thick lines. Familiarize yourself with how long a line you can draw for a given width, and try different color and width combinations to see how they look.

When starting on the mat (mount), hold the pen as nearly vertical as you feel comfortable with. Move the pen smoothly, but keep it at exactly the same angle to the mat (mount) from beginning to end of the line. Keep as accurately as possible to the start and finish points, although some leeway can be compensated for.

### Getting Down to Work
A single gold line around a mat (mount) may look attractive – but it is something everybody else does. Try a single gold line with a dark brown one on either side; it is much more eye-catching. A very attractive effect can be built up using several colors or tones, each one slightly darker than the

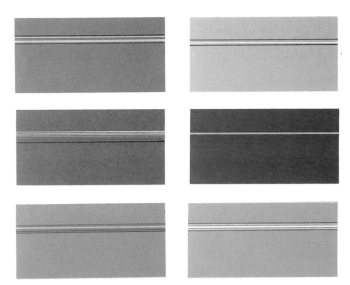

each subsequent one with the one preceding it. This is particularly useful when using the mat (mount) cutter as the straight-edge. To use the mat (mount) cutter as a guide for drawing ink lines, first cut two pieces of ¼ in (6 mm) timber, about 2 in (50 mm) square. Place one at either end of the cutter bar. Run the pen against the edge of the bar. There is no need to move the bar once the line has been drawn, simply turn the board round.

last. Start with a white line all around the mat (mount). Follow this with a cream one, then tan, medium brown, and so on, finishing with black; this gives the look of several mats (mounts) together, and is especially effective on darker-colored board.

There are a couple of important tips. First, when working on dark board, it is sometimes very difficult to see the finish point, especially if the pen is partly in the way. To avoid disaster, dot the finish point with the ink you are using – it makes it much easier to see. Second, when drawing several lines together, don't bother marking a point for each line, just mark the first one and learn to align

Try experimenting with different shapes at the corners of the mat (mount). Initial sketching of ideas, followed by trying out different shapes, is much easier to do first of all on graph paper. For anything other than straight lines, you will find a set of graphic designer's oval and circle templates indispensable. The few examples of corner shapes in the drawings on this page are just a beginning.

# WASH-LINE MATS (MOUNTS)

The next logical step after attaining this level of proficiency is the wash-line mat (mount). Just to remind you, a wash-line is simply a panel formed from a (variable) number of ink-lines, its center area containing a pale pastel shade of color that complements the subject being framed, usually a watercolor. The traditional method of wash-lining is as follows:

---

**Materials**

pencil
watercolors*
paint brushes†
straight edge
corner marking device
PVA paints
ruling pen

\* The watercolors are diluted with water (see Method).
† A selection of brushes of different widths is useful.

---

1 Lay out the panel on the mat (mount) in pencil.

2 Apply the watercolor wash. After establishing the required dilution of the color on a piece of scrap, prepare enough of this mixture to complete the whole panel.

3 Use clean water and a clean brush to wet the wash panel carefully.

4 Immediately after wetting, load your brush with the color mix and apply the wash. Keep the brush moving all the time it is in contact with the panel; keep within the pencil marks and work as quickly as is consistent with smooth application of color. Do not allow the color to form into pools. The moment of truth comes when you join up at the corner where you started. The

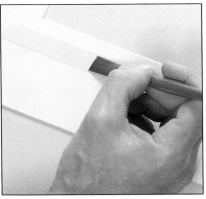

odds are that this will be partly dry by now. Take great care at this point, so that the join does not show. Only practice makes perfect, but the real trick is to keep the color consistent and apply it as quickly as possible without making mistakes. Another tip is to establish the width of panel that a given set of brushes will produce and stick to these widths.

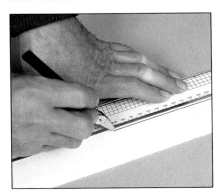

5 When the wash panel is completely dry, apply the complementary ink lines. Use varying dilutions of ink to soften the edges of the panel. The lines immediately adjoining the wash panel look best if they are pale and of the same color as the panel or in a complementary color.

Any number and combination of colors can be used, but you will find that the best and most enduringly attractive effects are produced by exercising restraint. An effective wash-line might contain three colors and a total of nine lines; this may sound a high number of ink lines, but it includes a double line on either side of the wash panel. The wash panel also looks at its best if there is a variation in the thickness of the ink lines, a thick line next to two thin ones and so on. A satisfyingly "finished" look is achieved if at least one of the two outermost lines is quite a dark one; this seems to hold the pattern of lines neatly together.

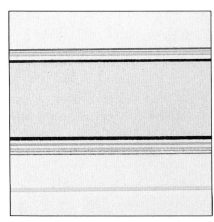

As with most artistic presentations, the finished article is very much dependent on personal taste, but you will generally know when you have achieved a good effect.

## T H E  D R Y  M E T H O D

As will now be evident, wash-line mats (mounts) are not a task for the novice or the fainthearted – but there is an easier way. It is called the "dry method" (and it also has a well-known brand name). It has been around for about 20 years, but for one reason or another has never received the acclaim it deserves.

The main ingredient of the process is a fine powder supplied in various typical wash-line colors. Unlike the traditional method, the ink-lines in this case are applied first. When these are dry, a simple foam brush is used to brush the powder into place within the panel formed by the lines. You

need to work fairly neatly to the lines and ensure the panel is liberally covered. Then you blow away the excess powder.

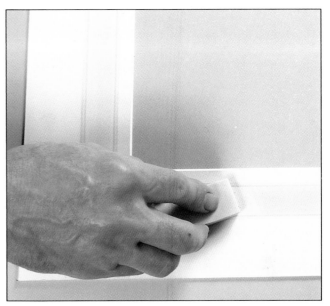

You now take the eraser supplied with the pack and, rubbing *only* within the panel, reduce the density of the powder until the correct paleness of color is achieved. The powder within the panel is rubbed into the fibers of the mat (mount) board, and so cannot be removed, whereas the excess powder outside the ink lines can be brushed away. The whole thing is simple and effective.

# NOVEL FINISHES

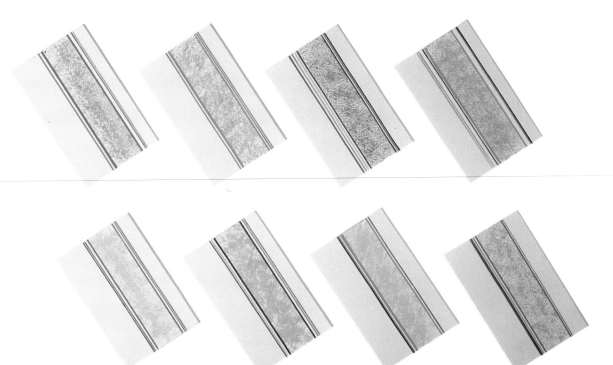

*I*t is a good idea to experiment with new ideas for decorative mat (mount) finishes. You can, for instance, achieve a deliberately "patchy" fill-in on a panel by varying the pressure on the brush while moving it along the panel. If this is performed uniformly, a very pleasing "cloud" effect can be achieved. Natural and synthetic sponges can also be used to produce a variety of pleasing effects. You can start by trying your hand at the following technique.

---

**Materials**

sponges*
watercolors or PVA paints
corner marking device
pencil
straight edge
stiff paper
Kraft paper, newspaper, base
paper[†]
solid glue stick
slim craft knife
protractor

* Natural sponges have an open texture; synthetic sponges give a closer stipple effect.
[†] Keep a selection of different papers to experiment on.

---

*1* Select a range of sponges. They must have a good texture and be of a reasonable size. About 1½ in (38 mm) diameter is about right for smaller jobs and a good large one about 6 in (150 mm) in diameter for bigger areas. Study the surface of the sponge and find the area where the texture is "spikiest."

*2* Spread diluted color (watercolor or PVA paint will do equally well) onto a white plate, and dab the sponge on it. Try the patterns on some scrap board.

*3* Change the wetness of the sponge and the dilution of the color and note the differences for future reference.

*4* Try various combinations of colors together – for instance green and red for a "garland of roses" effect; light blue and brown also look good together. When you have developed a sound application technique, use the technique on a full mat (mount).

*5* Mark out the board as if for a wash-line (i.e. a two-line panel). Join up the corner marks in pencil, thus forming a panel all around the cut opening.

*6* Cut a strip of stiff paper about 2 in (50 mm) wide, and prepare the color.

**7** Using the strip of paper as a cover, place it along one outer line of the panel. Stipple the sponge along this edge, then turn it around and repeat, so that the whole panel is covered with the first color. Repeat the process on the other three sides.

**8** Change the color and repeat the process.

The large sponge is used to cover larger areas – for instance, for "mottling" an entire mat (mount) – before or after cutting. It can also be used for creating your own mottled decorative papers. The resultant papers, when cut into strips and applied to the mat (mount), are most distinctive and, just as important, they are unique. Try different-colored base papers also for this, such as simple Kraft paper; you can also use newspaper to very good effect.

Stick the strips in place with a glue stick. Glue them by placing them face down on a piece of scrap board, applying the glue to the back of the strip; then smooth it into position on the mat (mount), using a faint pencil line as a guide. Miter each piece with a 45° cut as you apply it. A rough guess is good enough on pale boards, but you need to be more accurate on dark ones because the background will show through more.

There are, of course, dozens of commercially available designs of marbled and mottled papers. Attractive as many of them are, they are available to everybody. The ones you create are yours alone – and can be a source of pride.

# DECORATING UNDERMATS (MOUNTS)

When you have equipped yourself with a full set of PVA colors, think about painting undermats (mounts) when using a double mat (mount). You can mix exactly the color you need, you will always have the right color, and you will save a fortune by not having to stock different colors of board just for double mats (mounts). Moreover, you can use almost any board if you are painting it – it does not even have to be mat (mount) board. The bevel can be painted before or after cutting, so you also have the option of a white or colored bevel edge. The sponging mottled effect can also be used on undermats (mounts), and in the right circumstances is very attractive. Here is a form of decoration that will create an "antique gold-leaf" effect:

**Materials**

PVA paints in brownish-red, dark brown, pale green or gray and black
gilt varnish
stiff brush
straight edge
stiff paper
toothbrush
paintbrush
sponge

*1* Prepare a double mat (mount) in the usual way, the undermat (mount) preferably of thicker board.

*2* Paint the bevel and the ¼ in (6 mm) surrounding it in a brownish-red color to represent the clay base that old gold leaf was traditionally laid on.

*3* Stipple over this with dark brown fairly lightly; this provides the slightly "dirty" effect necessary. Allow this base coat to dry.

*4* Stipple gilt varnish on top of the base coat with a stiff brush, so that the red base shows through in patches.

*5* To finish off this effect, lay the straight edge of a scrap of stiff paper at right angles to the bevel at random intervals and stipple the gilt varnish half on the scrap and half on the mat (mount). This simulates the patches of denser gold where two leaves would either join or overlap.

*6* Mottle with very dilute pale green or gray, using a sponge, to simulate oxidation of the leaf.

*7* Dip a toothbrush in black paint and carefully spatter this on the bevel to provide "authentic" fly specks. The antique effect is now complete.

# GLASS MATS (MOUNTS)

*A* completely different approach to decorative effects is to use a glass mat (mount). This is an old method of producing a decorative border around a picture without having to use mat (mount) board. The decoration is carried out on the back of the glass, which will cover the whole picture.

**Materials**

glass
masking tape
pencil
straight edge
glass cutter
enamel paints*
paintbrush

* See step 4 for suitable colors, or use aerosol spray paints as described in Method.

*1*  Cut the glass for the finished size of the picture, plus borders. Thoroughly clean the glass.

*2*  Stick masking tape 2 in (50 mm) wide on the glass where the bevel would normally be, and mark its position all around with pencil.

*3*  Cut through the tape and remove the waste.

*4*  Paint the border directly on the glass with good quality enamel; dark colors work best on this type of mat (mount), particularly greens, blues,

and maroons. When the paint is dry, further marking may be done to form an inner border if required, perhaps in gold.

The result is a much denser color than is possible with mat (mount) board and is very effective for use with sporting prints or maritime subjects. To avoid making brush marks on the glass, use aerosol spray paints: those made for cars are ideal and are available in a very wide range of colors.

## HAND-DRAWN SHAPES

Much can be done by decorating mats (mounts) with hand-drawn shapes. Work inside a panel drawn in pencil. Gold and silver ink pens are now widely available in graphic art stores. Even the simplest shapes, outlined in gold ink and filled in with bright enamel colors and repeated all around the border, can be extremely effective and give that hand-finished look to your frames. Try to draw inspiration for the design from the subject being framed. For instance, this type of hand-decorated mat (mount) goes well with subjects such as Indian silk paintings or Egyptian papyrus. Invariably the subject has a clue for the decoration somewhere in the painting – perhaps a pattern or a combination of certain colors. Embellish the finished mat (mount) with suitable ink lines in complementary colors. Once you have the feel of these types of decoration, you will find that they won't really take

much longer to do than, say, a normal wash-line.

As with all adventurous ideas, there is no limit to what can be achieved. Don't be afraid to experiment.

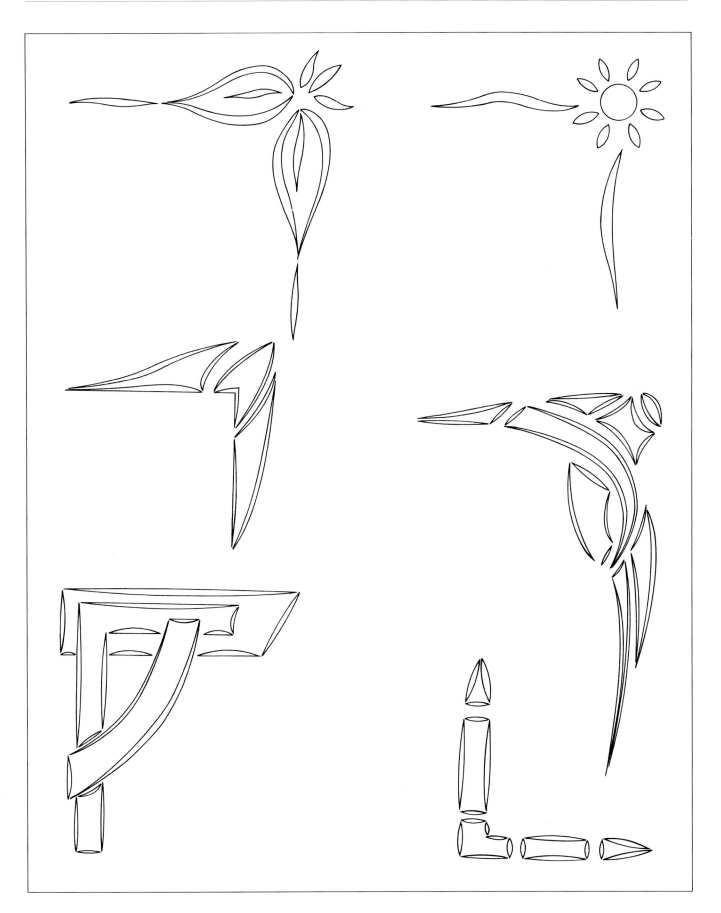

*A selection of designs for hand carving (see page 45) or hand drawing.*

# THE
# GLASS

# THE GLASS

Glass usually comes from the supplier in what are known as stock sheets. In Britain, the sheets are 6 × 4 ft (1.8 × 1.2 m) in size, which means they are both heavy and fragile. It is best to order it in half sheets, which are easier to handle and store. In the States, where glass is usually delivered by independent carriers, the sheet size is normally 4 × 3 ft (1.2 × 0.9 m).

## — THE GLASS-CUTTING AREA —

Keep your glass-cutting area separate from the rest of the workshop, and (out of consideration for your delivery man) as near to access from the street as possible. The glass-cutting bench needs to be about mid-thigh in height. It must be big enough to accommodate a sheet of glass and your tools – cutter, tape, T-square, and so on. As suggested already (*page 26*), cover the top with a good durable but resilient material such as foam-backed carpet (contract quality is preferable), and roll it over the front edge of the bench so it can act as a cushion when you are placing glass on the table.

it through 90 degrees, place it about a third of the way along its surface against the bench edge, then lower it to the bench top, supporting it firmly halfway along its length. Your glass-cutting tools include the following:

Oil-filled glass cutter
Two T-squares (medium and large sizes)
Long straight edge
Glass edging pliers
Tape measuring rule

When transferring glass from the rack to the bench, lift the sheet well clear of the floor. Turning

The long straight edge is for use on glass sheets too large for the T-squares to handle; it should preferably be fitted with suction pads. The pliers are for nibbling off those tiny, razor-sharp slivers of glass from the edge of a cut piece.

Keep a bin close to your bench. You may be offered one free by your local scrap-glass dealer (or cullet merchant, to give him his traditional name). Always keep the top of your cutting bench free of glass fragments; half the mistakes made when cutting glass could be avoided by keeping the bench top well swept. Get into the habit of sweeping it before each cutting session – you are always too busy afterwards.

Stack the glass vertically against a stout support, preferably on a purpose-built rack. Keep the base of the rack scrupulously clean; much damage to glass is caused by stacking it on waste fragments. Never stack glass perfectly: stagger the sheets, so that the end edge of any individual sheet is not flush with that of its neighbor on either side. Sometimes a vacuum forms between two sheets, and it is almost impossible to separate them if they

are lined up perfectly. Allow each alternate sheet to overlap its immediate neighbors by about ¼ in (6 mm) to allow you to grip them firmly.

## GLASS TYPES

Glass comes in various thicknesses and different grades according to its method of manufacture. In the United States glass comes in two thicknesses: single strength, which is approximately ³⁄₁₆ in or 2.5 mm thick, and double strength. In the U.K. standard glass is available in 2 mm, 3 mm and 4 mm thicknesses.

Two different methods of manufacture produce sheet glass and float glass. Sheet glass is made in the traditional way by vertical manufacture, a process which tends to produce wavy lines within the structure of the glass. Single strength or 2 mm sheet glass is suitable for general, unspecialized framing of pictures up to 20 × 16 in (500 × 400 mm) in size. Float glass is made by the modern method of glass manufacture, in which the glass sets horizontally and therefore finds its own level, thus minimizing the possibility of waviness. Single strength or 2 mm float glass is good for all but the most critical work and can be used for frames up to 4 feet (1.2 m) square.

Depending on where the glazed image is to hang, you may wish to use non-reflective glass.

There are many views on the comparative merits of non-reflective and plain glass. The non-reflective type is generally around 25% more expensive than plain glass, and this limits demand for it in certain types of business, and also makes it less attractive to the hobbyist. In view of the quite bogus conviction in some quarters that non-reflective glass is intrinsically superior, it may be helpful to explain the real, and important, distinctions between the two types.

The technical description of the non-reflective type is "diffused-reflection glass." This property has the effect that the greater the distance an object is from the glass, the more diffused (out of focus) it will appear when viewed from the other side of the glass. Thus, it puts a severe restriction on the use of multiple mats (mounts) in picture frames.

On the other hand, its capacity to minimize reflections from the viewer's side of the glass makes it invaluable in places such as large reception areas and any location where most of the light will be coming from behind the viewer.

There are again various grades of non-reflective glass, and new types appear on the market regularly. At the least expensive end is a non-reflective glass, which should not be used with a mat (mount) as it will tend to "gray" the image. It is most commonly used for photographs. The next grade can be used with a double mat (mount) without distortion. After these comes a range of American-made specialty glasses designed for reflection control and protection against the ultra-violet light, which causes colors to fade in time. At the top end of this range, for framing where conservation is a critical factor, is a glass which will absorb most of the ultra-violet light and cut surface reflection to a minimum with very little distortion of the art.

All types of glass can be cleaned in the usual way (*see page 67*).

If you have occasion to order thicker glass, make sure to stack it separately. Likewise keep your stocks of plain and non-reflective glass in separate positions.

### *Other Glazing Materials*

Clear polystyrene sheets are sometimes used for framing. The quality of its appearance is inferior to glass, and it is possible that it will yellow with age, but it has a use in various specific situations, for example, where safety is more important than appearance. It can be written on with a felt-tipped pen, therefore, is useful for glazing notices where there is likely to be a regular change of information. It is cut with a heavy craft knife.

### CUTTING GLASS

There are two keys to good glass cutting: confidence and technique. A good glass-cutting instrument helps, too, but is not absolutely vital. The oil-filled type is recommended, purely because it lasts much longer than the six-wheeled type that you buy at the local hardware store, and so it is far more economical in the long run.

If you lack confidence when cutting glass, things inevitably go wrong. Many people assume that the harder you press with the cutter, the more effective is the cut. The reverse is true. Practice on scrap glass and you may be surprised at how little pressure you need to make an effective and easily separated cut. Remember this pressure and be aware of it all the time when cutting.

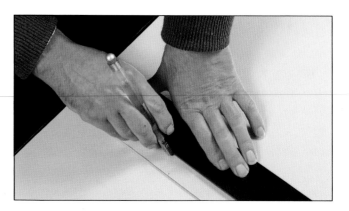

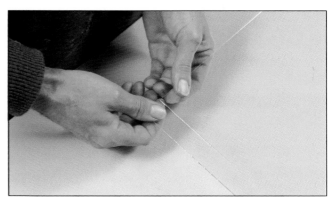

This, incidentally, is another reason why oil-filled cutters are better. The action that feeds the tiny amount of oil from the hollow handle through the head to the cutting wheel consists of a spring-controlled movement of a tiny fraction of an inch between the head and the handle. The pressure required to activate the oil flow is also the pressure required to make an effective cut – and it is very light indeed. After the cut is made, it requires minimal persuasion to make the glass part with that satisfying "ping." Merely lifting the glass with two fingers of both hands underneath and thumbs on top on either side of the line is usually all that is necessary. Press upward with both fingers at the same time as pressing downward and outward with the thumbs. Once you have developed this technique, you will soon find that the seemingly fiddly job of trimming, say, $\frac{1}{12}$ in (2 mm) off the end of a piece you have cut slightly large holds no terrors for you any more.

Confidence will usually follow successful practice. But it may help to indicate some of the commoner errors in technique. Unsuccessful cutting is most commonly due to inconsistency of pressure along the length of the cut. This generally results in refusal of the glass to part at all and enforces re-cutting, another undesirable practice. Re-cutting may make the glass break in the correct place, but it will give it an unsightly splintered edge.

If the cut is too long to make in one continuous stroke, make certain that the two cuts do not overlap. That error is one of the causes of glass "running off" (breaking at right angles to the cut line). A second cut beginning exactly where the first cut finished is ideal; but even a small uncut space of perhaps $\frac{1}{20}$ in (1 mm) between your cuts is preferable to an overlap.

Keep the cutter as upright as you can feel comfortable with. This ensures that the wheel remains fully in contact with the glass throughout the length of your cutting stroke. Start as near as possible to the top edge of the glass, and run off the edge of the glass at the end of the stroke and onto the base of the "T"-square. Break out the cut by lifting the glass and applying slight downward pressure on either side of the cut. If the cut is a good one, the glass will separate effortlessly.

Always allow a reasonable clearance when marking out the glass for cutting; $\frac{1}{16}$ in (1.5 mm) less than the width and length of the frame is about right. But remember to allow for the distance between the edge of the glass-cutter head and the center of the cutting wheel; this is usually about $\frac{1}{12}$ in (2 mm).

## GLASS CLEANERS

There are many good proprietary glass cleaners on the market, but you will find that a 50/50 mixture of denatured alcohol and water works very well indeed. Use a lint-free cloth for cleaning, and if possible finish off the underside with an anti-static duster; this helps to discourage accumulation of those little bits of dirt that inevitably appear after a picture has been assembled and taped up.

When fitting the glass, assemble all the component parts of the framing job and lay the glass on top. Place the frame over these after an inspection for any unwanted "intruders." Then pick up the complete unit and turn it over for assembly.

*The difference between reflective and non-reflective glass. The slight texture of the non-reflective glass is visible over the picture.*

# THE
# MOLDING

# TIMBER TYPES

*T*his chapter covers different kinds of timber moldings used in picture framing; how they are made; and how they are decorated by machine and by hand.

The most important first step is to select the best type of timber for the particular moldings you require. In general, the timber must be stable, free from defects, and must not warp or twist. Next, you must ensure that the timber can be mitered easily and will accept joining pins or wedges inserted by traditional or modern methods.

Over the past 40 or 50 years, three timbers have established themselves as most suitable for picture-frame moldings; two of them are hardwoods and one a softwood.

## HARDWOODS

*The three main hardwoods used in framing, from left to right: ramin; pine; obeche*

### *Ramin*

**Origin**: Indonesia and Malaysia
Botanical name: *Gonystylus bancanus*

Mature ramin trees are up to 60 ft (18 m) high, but their main stems are usually no more than 2 ft (600 mm) in diameter. They grow in swampy forests and are found in abundance in the swamps of Sarawak, notably in the Rajang river delta. The timber is a uniformly creamy white and has a fine, even texture combined with a shallowly interlocked grain.

This is an excellent timber for both cutting and machining and gives a good quality machined surface that accepts most finishes. The finished surface is characterized by a smooth, closed-grain appearance. Ramin is widely used in the picture-frame industry for both composition and on-the-wood finish moldings. Its one disadvantage is that it is very prone to shrink, even after thorough drying in a kiln. So avoid using ramin moldings wider than 1½ in (38 mm): the larger the molding, the greater the variation that will be encountered when you attempt to miter and join corners.

In today's political climate, ramin is becoming difficult to import into Europe and North America in lumber form. The producing countries are being encouraged by their governments to export the timber already machined as component parts, including machined moldings.

### *Obeche or Wawa*

**Origin**: West Africa
Botanical name: *Triplochiton scleroxylon*

Obeche comes from Nigeria and wawa comes from Ghana, but in the timber trade the term obeche is used for both. It is one of the commonest trees of this region of West Africa. The logs vary from 18 in to 6 ft (450 to 1800 mm) in diameter and are anything from 12 to 25 ft (3.5 to 7.5 m) long. The wood is a creamy white to straw color and the grain is slightly interlocked with an open texture.

Like ramin, this is a good timber for cutting and machining. The finished machined surface is not quite as good as ramin as it has a slightly more open grain, but it is of an acceptable standard and is suitable for many of the finishes required.

There are many grades of obeche. Make sure to buy only the best, which are known as F.A.S. grades. Most grades are prone to some defect caused by grub hole and pin worm. All these grades are treated prior to shipment abroad, ensuring that all forms of beetle and worm are destroyed, but their holes will still be present in the timber. Any holes still showing after the timber has been machined to section can be filled with a proprietary wood filler before you apply any finishing process. Obeche is less prone to shrinkage than ramin and so it is suitable for any size of profile.

### Other Hardwoods

Other hardwoods that are suitable for use in picture-frame moldings are the American and Canadian hardwoods – oak, ash, cherry, maple, and occasionally basswood and poplar, although the last two are rarely used outside the United States. These timbers can be stained and then clear-lacquered or coated with tinted lacquer in order to enhance the natural beauty and color of the grain in the finished molding (*see page 75*).

## SOFTWOODS

### Pine

**Origin**: Sweden, Finland, and Soviet Union
Botanical name: *Pinus*

This timber is generally admired for its knotty content and distinctive grain, and it is used for a different although slightly more limited range of finishes than ramin or obeche. Pine trees grow very fast, tall, and straight in cold conditions, whereas ramin and obeche trees need a warm climate and take many years to mature before they are ready for felling. As with obeche, there are many grades of pine. Generally the top grade, known as the "unsorted grade," is found to be the best for picture-frame moldings.

*From left to right: Japanese oak; Ramin sarawak; Canadian basswood; African obeche; Canadian yellow cedar; Russian pine*

# MANUFACTURED FINISHES

*T*he boards are treated in the following manner to produce the wide range of manufactured moldings now available.

### KILN DRYING

Timber for picture-frame moldings must be kiln-dried to reduce its moisture content to between 7 and 10 per cent. The process is as follows:

Single boards or sections of timber are placed side by side in layers to form a stack; the layers are separated by sticks about ¾ in (19 mm) thick to enable the air to circulate around each piece of timber. The stacks are then loaded into the kiln for drying. The temperature within the kiln is set to 250°–275°F (120°–140°C).

Steam is pumped into the kiln to prevent the high temperature from breaking down the structure of the timber, which would cause it to split and bend. The heat and steam are separately controlled. Large fans reverse the air-flow direction hourly, making sure that the timber is dried evenly all around.

Once the material is dry and removed from the kiln, it must be kept under cover and at a constant working temperature during the rest of the production processes, otherwise the moldings will pick up moisture again. The kilning process can take anything from 36 hours to several days, depending on the species and conditions of the timber.

### SELECTING AND CUTTING THE TIMBER

Most timber on arrival in the country will be in packs of boards which have painted or gritty ends.

The gritty ends of the boards are cross cut to prevent the profile cutters being damaged by the grit or paint particles and causing marks to appear on the machined surface. Cross cutting ensures that the boards in each pack are cut to the same length, which makes handling much easier.

The boards are then ripped down to produce pieces of the correct width to feed into the profile cutter. Sections must be cut accurately from the board to allow just enough material to produce the finished profile.

### LAMINATED MOLDINGS

Sometimes two or more pieces of timber of different sizes are cut and joined to make one section by gluing and laminating the pieces together.

This is done for various reasons. One is that the different tensions in the separate pieces of timber react together and so help to keep the composite section much straighter than would be possible by using a solid piece of timber. Another reason is to reduce the total amount of timber used in a given profile by reducing the amount machined to dust. A third reason, especially when using pine, is to arrange the grain patterns on the two pieces to give a pleasing effect; this is often impossible to achieve with a single piece of timber.

## CUTTER GRINDING AND PROFILING

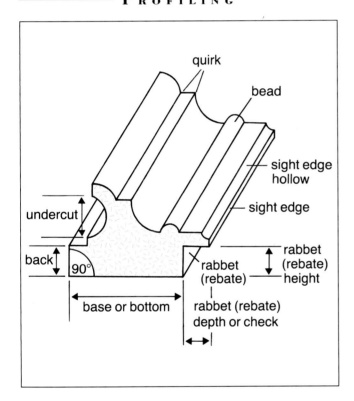

The next stage is to select a molding profile and to prepare the cutting irons to produce it. But before dealing with this we need to familiarize ourselves with the names of the various parts of the end section of a profile (*see drawing*).

With today's machinery, the accuracy of cutter grinding and the quality of the finished machined surface are extremely high. Master templates are produced by accurate scribing of the profile onto a piece of ½ in (2 mm) steel. The shape is then cut

out with a hacksaw and finished off using fine metal files. The master template is then used to reproduce the profile onto the cutters by copy grinding, thus ensuring accuracy and continuity of profile for any future batches. These operations in the machine shop are carried out by skilled craftsmen. The piece of timber progresses through a molding machine, with an array of cutting heads which gradually produce the finished profile.

It is vital that the base of the molding is machined to form a right-angle with the back of the molding, otherwise it will be very difficult to ensure accurate mitering of the finished product.

This stage in the manufacture of a picture-frame molding is critical because the quality and finish of the machined timber contributes largely to the final product. Mistakes made at this part of the operation can rarely be corrected.

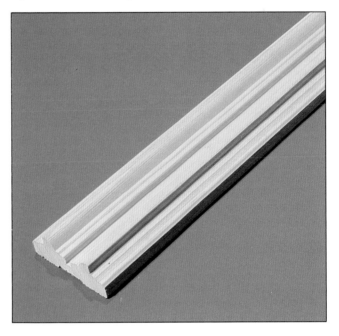

Some smaller profiles can be produced as fixed doubles. This greatly speeds the cutting operation and makes feeding the moldings through the machines used in later processes much easier, especially with large-volume runs. The double moldings are later rabbeted (rebated) and split into singles.

There is an almost infinite variety of end profiles for moldings. A few representative types are identified in the drawings overleaf.

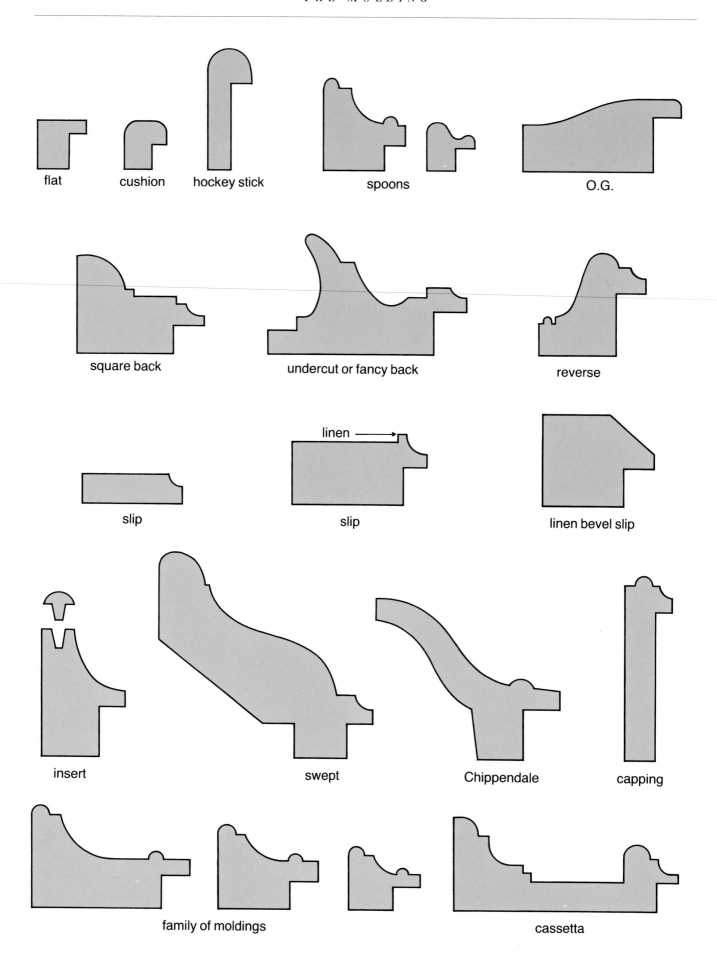

flat

cushion

hockey stick

spoons

O.G.

square back

undercut or fancy back

reverse

slip

linen →

slip

linen bevel slip

insert

swept

Chippendale

capping

family of moldings

cassetta

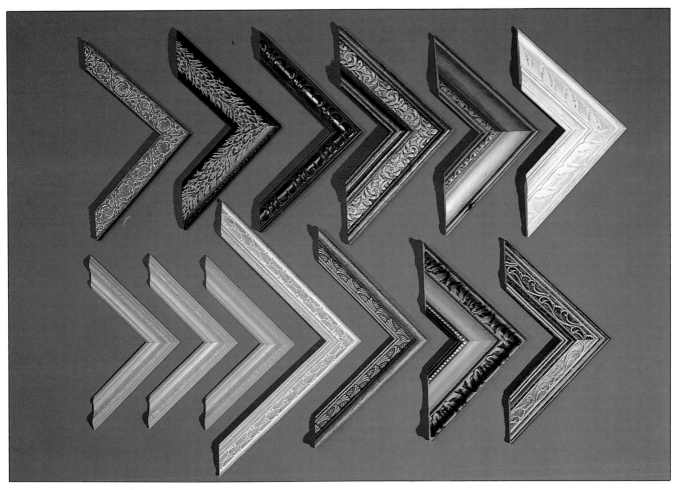

*Embossed moldings with a variety of different finishes.*

## EMBOSSED MOLDINGS

This type of molding is produced at the whitewood stage – that is, after the basic profile has been produced by the cutters. The molding is embossed by passing it under an engraved metal roller heated by a gas jet. The combination of heat and pressure burns the design engraved on the roller into the timber.

In general, obeche is the best timber to use for embossed moldings: ramin is too hard for a good impression to be made, and pine tends to splinter and crack under pressure.

## GRAINING

As mentioned earlier, one of the attractions of pine for the picture framer is its natural grain. The effect of the grain can be enhanced by feeding the

*Moldings treated to enhance the grain.*

molding through a series of rotating or fixed wire brushes. This has the effect of removing the pith from between the layers of grain and of giving a "distressed" character to the molding surface; this makes an interesting base for applying other finishing processes.

## PAINTING AND LACQUERING

Once the physical shape of the molding has been established by the cutters and, possibly, also by embossing, it is ready for coloring. A very large number of effects can be created using an equally large number of materials applied in a variety of ways. The two main methods of applying the materials are vacuum coating and spray coating.

### Vacuum Coating

This method is used to apply water-based stains, paints, and lacquers that contain no solvents. The process consists of passing the molding through two openings in opposite sides of an otherwise sealed box. The openings are shaped to the exact contour of the molding to ensure a tight fit. A vacuum pump is connected to the box and the pressure inside the box is reduced to well below that of the atmosphere. At the same time, the material, stain, or lacquer is pumped into a series of baffles inside

*Lengths of molding on drying racks.*

the box. As a result, the timber effectively passes through a swirling, atomized bath of the material, which coats the timber all over its exposed surfaces. The timber is then placed on specially built racks for the coating to dry.

With most operations, it is necessary to put more than one coat of material on the molding in order to build up the finished surface. In the simplest case, it would be one coat of stain to color the timber followed by three or four coats of lacquer to build up the surface and produce a good sheen. As with nearly all coating processes, the timber molding is buffed between coats to remove surface blemishes and key the surface for subsequent coats.

### Spray Coating

This method is used to apply solvent-based materials to the timber. The spray guns are fixed in position and the moldings are fed past them in order to be coated. Up to five or six separate coats are applied to build up the surface required, the moldings being buffed between each coat.

## APPLIED FINISHES FOR MOLDINGS

The range of materials that can be applied by either of the methods described above is almost endless and new ones are constantly being developed. The following are some of the more common ones.

**Clear Lacquers**   Lacquer is a transparent material used to give a protective layer to the molding, so that it can be handled and wiped clean without affecting the surface. Lacquers can give a matt, satin or gloss finish and they are applied over natural wood or over a decorated surface.

**Tinted Lacquers**   Clear lacquers containing small amounts of concentrated inks which color the lacquer without making it opaque.

**Enamel Paints**   Solid colors used mainly on composition moldings to give a glossy, smooth finish.

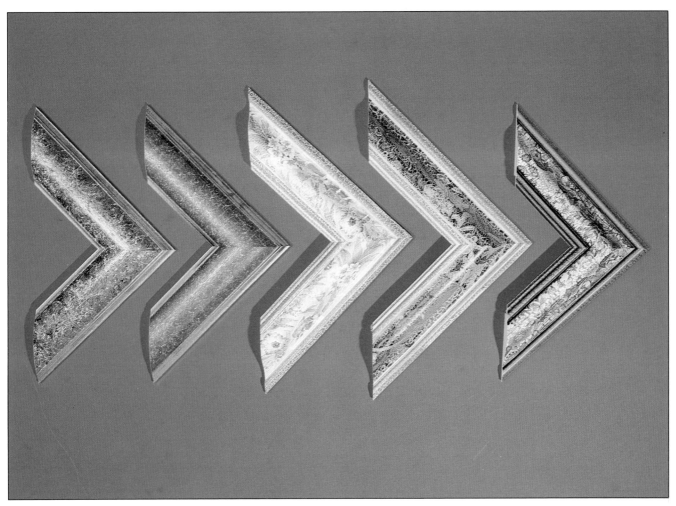

*The crackle effect on different decorations.*

**Gilts**   Finely ground gold or silver powders which are mixed with clear lacquers to give a gold or silver base on which to apply other processes.

**Crackle Lacquers**   A system in which a thick coat of applied lacquer cracks on drying into a series of hairline fractures to give the "crazed" effect similar to a ceramic glaze.

**Spider Web**   This material forms into long, thin strands which give the effect of a colored cobweb pattern on the molding surface.

**Patina**   A type of lacquer that, on drying, leaves a surface powder which can be rubbed off. The trick is to rub off the powder only in certain areas; this gives a light and dark, or two-tone, effect which is then sealed with a coat of clear lacquer.

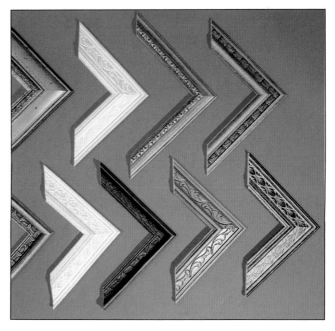

*A further selection of embossed moldings. Note the patina on the light woods.*

*Intricate relief designs produced by adding wood pulp to the timber.*

## DECORATIVE MOLDINGS

This type of molding provides a decorative finish of much greater depth and definition of detail than is possible with embossing. In the past, this kind of decoration was produced as a separate process from a substance called *mast*, which was similar in consistency to raw bread dough. The mast was formed into a 10 ft (3 m) sausage shape on a length of flat steel sheeting, and an engraved roller was drawn along it to produce the decorative effect. The pressing was later lifted off the sheeting and laid onto the molding in the required position.

Wood pulp has nowadays replaced mast, and advances in machinery mean that it can now be fed directly onto the surface of the molding from an extrusion machine and passed under the engraved roller in one operation. Once the material has set, the molding can be finished by any of the previously described operations.

*Adding and impressing the wood pulp.*

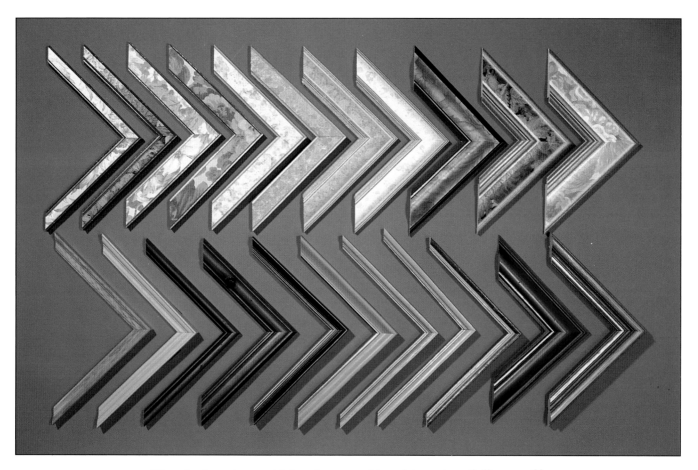

*The selections above and below show something of the variety of effects possible
with machine-finished processes.*

## MACHINE FINISHING

There are so many machine-finishing processes
that it would be impossible to describe them all.
The following are just a few of the basic
techniques used.

A typical example of machine finishing is a
simple satin-lacquered or two-tone molding which
requires only a colored line or gold-foil bead along
the sight edge or hollow.

The gold bead is generally applied by the Folien
method, in which a strip of gold foil attached to a
clear plastic carrier is pressed onto the molding by
a heated silicon roller. The heat and pressure
release the foil from its carrier, and it adheres to
the molding. Depending on the size and shape of
the roller, foil can be applied to any area of the
molding surface. Apart from gold, silver, and
bronze, a variety of solid colors, and even floral or
patterned designs, can be applied by this method.

# HAND FINISHES

## Staining and Painting

Molding can be hand-finished in a variety of ways. This section deals with the four types of finish most commonly used in picture framing: stains, paint, gesso, and gilding.

Most hand finishing will be done on new timber moldings. Raw wood needs to be prepared and the grain filled, as described below.

On the other hand, you may wish to apply a finish to an old frame that has been decorated before. How you do this will depend on the nature of the previous decoration. It may be paint, gilt, french polish, or something else. **Be very careful that your work over this surface will not harm the original**, if it is at all valuable. If you decide that the finish on your frame has no intrinsic value and the new work over it is justified, then the original finish should be stripped. If you are carrying work out on someone else's frame, it might be worth obtaining a signed disclaimer relieving you of responsibility, if the molding is later found out to have been "valuable."

Use either an appropriate solvent on the finish or a proprietary stripper. Water can be used for removing gesso, but this is not recommended as the gesso is likely to have been the preparation for a beautiful surface finish that can possibly be conserved or restored. For french polish, use denatured alcohol (methylated spirits); for paint, paint stripper. Once you have stripped the surface, you are back to the original wood and you can build up again from there.

If you have decided to leave the original surface intact, but it needs to be cleaned, use mineral spirits (white spirit) to remove any wax and grease. It may be necessary to use two or three washes to clean the surface thoroughly. To clean out wax from deep moldings, use a suede brush or an old toothbrush dipped in the spirits.

### — STAINING AND POLISHING —

Staining the molding can enhance the beauty of the wood grain, and a great variety of colors and finishes can be achieved. Polishing adds a final protection to the wood and produces a "mid-sheen" finish to the frame.

Three types of stain are discussed here: water, oil, and chemical.

## W A T E R   S T A I N S

The coloring agents for water stains are either water-soluble aniline dyes or vegetable or mineral dyes. Water stains can be tricky to handle as they do not penetrate the wood as readily as oil stains, resulting in an uneven finish. Oily timbers, such as teak, are particularly prone to this problem. Beech is the best timber to use. Water stains need to be sealed, once they have been applied. Proceed as follows:

### Warning

All stains are potentially toxic. Be particularly careful not to inhale dry, powdered aniline dyes. Do not lick brushes that have been used in stains, and wash your hands carefully, especially after using chemical stains. Be aware that all solvents can dry out your skin, and prolonged use can cause irritation. However, provided they are handled carefully, these materials can produce wonderful results, with no danger to the user.

### Materials

water stains and water-soluble aniline dyes
oil stains
cotton rags
sandpaper
shellac or french polish
denatured alcohol (methylated spirits), to use as solvent for shellac
soft brush for applying shellac/french polish
clear wax furniture polish*
wood dye
polyurethane varnish, gloss or matt
mineral spirits (white spirit)
soft cloth for applying wax
wool rag for final burnishing

* Use a good quality furniture polish in cake form, not a spray.

*1* Water on the surface of wood will raise the grain and roughen the surface. Before staining, dampen the surface of the molding, leave to dry, then sandpaper it smooth. Repeat this as often as necessary, stopping only when the grain no longer swells when it is dampened.

*2* To apply the stain, use a rag rather than a brush. It is difficult to control the flow of stain with a brush. A cotton rag is the best kind to use. Have an old rag handy for wiping off surplus

stain. Dip the cotton rag in the stain, then draw along the grain in even strokes, aiming the overlaps in the "quirks" of the molding (*see page 73*). Wipe off the excess stain immediately with another rag. Be sure to let the first coat dry completely before applying a second.

Note that areas of stain that are too light can be re-stained. Where the stain is too dark, it can be removed using the appropriate solvent (water for a water stain; mineral spirits/white spirit for an oil stain). Always allow the timber to dry before re-staining.

*3* To seal a water stain, first make sure that the surface is thoroughly dry and smooth. Brush on a thin coat of shellac or french polish. This dries extremely fast, so you cannot go back on your work. Use a good quality soft brush and draw the polish along in long, even strokes.

*4* When the shellac is dry, apply a thin coat of polyurethane varnish. Thin the varnish with mineral spirits (white spirit) until it is like milk. The varnish is used as a seal but does not need to be hard-wearing.

*5* For a gloss finish, apply a second coat of gloss polyurethane varnish, again thinned like milk. For a matt finish, apply a second coat of matt polyurethane varnish, as above.

*6* When the varnish is quite dry, polish it with wax furniture polish, using a soft rag. This has the effect of repelling dust particles and giving a marvelous sheen, which can be burnished again and again.

### Alternative Finishes

You can omit the sealing stage and wax directly onto the stain; this will give a duller finish. When shellac or french polish is used, it fills the grain; the more coats that are applied, the more the grain is filled and the smoother and silkier the surface becomes. If this stage is left out, the wax will soak straight into the wood, and the grain will remain open. The polish can be tinted with a wood dye.

### Oil Stains

The coloring matter for these usually comes from coal tar or bitumen products, and tints can be added using other oil-soluble dyes. These products can be thinned with mineral spirits (white spirit). Oil stains penetrate the wood well, producing rich colors such as mahogany, walnut, and black; the colors are easier to apply, but are not as permanent as water stains. They will fade with time. They tend to be used on hard woods, and take longer to dry.

Apply in the same way as for a water stain, leaving at least a couple of hours between coats. To seal, first leave the molding for a day or two to dry completely, then seal it with shellac, as for a water stain.

### Chemical Stains

Chemical stains must be treated with extreme caution by the amateur because they are toxic. Their application is specific: potassium permanganate darkens pine and oak; potassium bichromate turns mahogany a rich red; blue or green coppers produce amazing effects on oak.

Chemical stains produce colors by reacting with

*Examples of the different stains – from left to right: shellaced water stain; chemical stain; oil stain.*

acids present in the timber rather than by impregnating color, as is the case with aniline dyes. They provide a wealth of opportunity for further study, once other staining techniques have been mastered.

## PAINTING

Oil paints include decorator's paints, such as flat oil, eggshell, and gloss paints. The most suitable for picture frames are flat oil or trade eggshell preceded by a coat of undercoat.

Signwriter's paint is fast-drying oil paint. This paint is heavy in pigment, will dry matt, and can be obtained from good signwriters' suppliers. The average drying time is two hours. If you want a shiny finish, apply one coat of mid-sheen polyurethane varnish and, when it is quite dry, follow it with a thin application of a good wax furniture polish in cake form (not a spray).

## COLOR-MATCHING

Most oil paints darken slightly on drying, especially if they contain a good quantity of white pigment, so you must allow for this if you are trying to match an existing color. A test can be made by painting a dab on a plain piece of white paper and heating it very carefully over a flame for a few seconds. This will drive the solvents off and you will soon see the tone of the dry paint. Acrylic colors change less than oils on drying, but it will pay you to test a patch of these, too, before deciding on your mix.

To match colors in oil, start with the closest flat-oil or eggshell color you can find to the base color, or use off-white. Err on the light side, as paint can more easily be darkened than lightened. A tube color, such as an artist's oil color, can be used to alter the tone, but it will need to be blended in as this type of paint is much thicker than decorator's paint. Blend it in with a palette knife on a tile, using a small quantity of the base color. Adding color darkens the paint; so go easy and add it very carefully, matching it all the time to the original. Be wary when using black; it will not always darken in the way you might expect, and can change a color value considerably.

It is also useful to consider whether a color needs to be warmer or cooler. You can often get a better match this way than by concentrating on the exact shade required. A color can be toned down or made more brown by adding a tiny quantity of its opposite. Thus, a little red added to green will tone the green down. Adding Payne's Gray will darken most colors.

Use the following method for painting and decorating a frame:

---

### Materials

oil paints*
artist's tube oil colors
hogshair or bristle brushes, for flat painting of solid color
soft brushes, for detailed painting of lines or motifs
sandpaper
mineral spirits (white spirit)
white undercoat
cotton rag
clean cans for decanting paint into
white tiles for mixing colors

palette knife
mid-sheen polyurethane varnish
good quality wax furniture polish in cake form
transparent or scumble glaze
decorating aids: natural or synthetic sponge, cheesecloth, comb, stiff brush, paper†

* See text for types of paints.
† The decorating aids are suggestions only, as explained in Method.

---

*1* A bare wood surface needs to be prepared for painting. Fill any holes with wood filler and, when it has dried, rub it smooth with sandpaper, making sure the whole surface is clean, dry, and very smooth. If oil paint is to be used as a base for glazing or further decoration, make a primer coat using 50:50 flat oil or eggshell paint and mineral spirits (white spirit). Thereafter add only enough spirits to enable the paint to flow well.

*2* Oil-based paint generally needs stirring and is best decanted into another container. Try to judge exactly how much you will need for the job. Do not pour left-over paint back into the can as it will have collected dust.

*3* When the paint has been applied to the surface along one length of the frame, remove the excess by dragging the brush along the molding in even strokes from end to end. Then move to the next length. Allow each coat to dry thoroughly before applying the next, and be careful not to leave drips or runs in the paint. Once a solid color is achieved, there is no need to apply more paint.

*4* A glaze can be used to create finishes such as sponging, dragging, stippling, rag-rolling, combing, and so on. Mix one part of the transparent glaze with one part of mineral spirits (white spirit) and up to one part of white undercoat. If you want a tinted glaze, add a little artist's oil color.

*5* The glaze dries fast, but on a small picture frame you should have enough time to produce your chosen finish before the glaze becomes unworkable. Large frames can be glazed and finished one length at a time. Splashes can be wiped off easily with a rag dipped in mineral spirits (white spirit).

   If the glaze mixture is to be stored overnight, keep it covered with plastic wrap. This will prevent loss of moisture and formation of a hard skin on the surface.

*6* The range of effects that can be achieved is enormous, so experiment on scrap pieces of molding first. For instance, use a sponge to speckle the color of the molding. Moisten the sponge with mineral spirits

(white spirit) and wring it out. Dip it into a saucer of the tinted glaze and apply it to the frame. For best results and maximum texture, keep the sponge as dry as possible. Alternatively, paint the frame thinly with the tinted glaze and follow this around with the sponge, creating your texture.

*7* A cheesecloth can be used in a similar way. Moisten it and crumple it up before applying to the molding.

*8* Try other media for different textures and finishes to the tinted glaze, such as a comb, a stiff brush, or crumpled paper.

*9* Another finish that is quick and easy to apply is the "spatter" technique. Dip a brush into a saucer of the tinted glaze, so that it is lightly loaded, then tap it against another brush or against your extended finger, allowing the paint to spatter onto a sheet of newspaper. Practice this effect until you can control the amount of spatter and are happy with the results, then carry out the spattering onto the chosen frame. If a darkish-brown tinted glaze is used, the results will imitate flyspecks, wormholes, and general ageing remarkably well. This is a technique popular with Italian framers.

Different glaze finishes can be applied to a wide variety of moldings. Small, detailed moldings are best given a simple finish, a wiped or dragged finish sufficing to add depth and interest to the surface. On a wide molding, more elaborate work can be carried out, especially if the frame is flat in the center. This type is known as a *cassetta* frame (*see page 74*); it originated in Renaissance Italy and its wide center panel lends itself to decoration of every kind. An antique example is shown above.

## CLEANING BRUSHES

### Oil Paint

Wipe excess paint from brushes with a rag and rinse them thoroughly in successive washes of mineral spirits (white spirit) until no color comes out. Smaller artist's brushes used for oil paint can be kept greased either with petroleum jelly or in engine oil. When required for use, rinse them first in clean spirits.

Decorator's brushes should be cleaned thoroughly after each job. When all traces of paint have been removed, wash out the mineral spirits (white spirit) by thoroughly working the brush in washing-up liquid and hot water. Rinse, wrap the brush-head in newspaper, and leave it to dry. An aluminum device called a brush keep enables you to suspend the heads of smaller brushes in mineral spirits (white spirit) or kerosene (paraffin). This saves a lot of cleaning time and is kind to the brushes, but do not leave the brushes suspended in the solvent for days at a time, as prolonged emersion may cause them to deteriorate.

### Acrylic Paint

Never allow your brush to dry when it is coated with acrylic paint; acrylics are soluble in water only while they are wet. Keep the brush wet at all times, and wash it out in soap and water when you have finished work. It may be possible to revive a brush in denatured alcohol (methylated spirits), if it has hardened with paint.

## CLEANING DECORATING AIDS

### Sponge

A natural sea sponge or a synthetic sponge is used for creating speckled effects with paint. Wash it as you would a paint brush.

### Muslin Cloths

These are used to create a surface texture, either flat or bunched up. If left in a heap when covered with oil paints or glaze, they can be a dangerous fire risk: rags can ignite spontaneously. Clean and wash out after use. During a decorating session, do not leave them lying around: hang them up, so that air can circulate freely around.

# GESSO

*G*esso (the Italian for "gypsum") is a medium used in the decoration of furniture and in making bas-reliefs. The earliest-known examples of its use date back to ancient Egyptian times, and the materials and techniques involved have changed hardly at all over 2,000 years.

Gesso consists of two ingredients: gelatin glue, derived from the skins and bones of animals and known as rabbitskin glue; and chalk (calcium carbonate), which for our purposes is available as best gilder's whiting.

The glue is bought in dry, usually granulated form and reconstituted for use. Soak it overnight, using one part of granules to 15 parts of cold water; then heat the swollen particles thoroughly until they have melted and the glue is of even consistency. *Do not boil* or it will be useless. While the glue is hot, gently add a quantity of sifted whiting to it, mixing it in with a hogshair brush only when the liquid glue will not hold any more whiting. The mixture should be the consistency of thin cream.

This will give you a gesso which can be used for preparing a raw wood surface. It is the oldest and most effective grain filler yet invented, being flexible, economical, and, once mastered, very versatile. The gesso will set when cold and can be kept in a refrigerator for future use. It will keep for a couple of weeks.

Apply it to the wood as follows:

---

**Materials**

saucepan for heating gesso
stoneware jar to hold warm gesso
hogshair brushes
soft shaving brush or cottonwool
cotton rag
sandpaper (320-grit)
materials for making textures:
scrim, screwdriver, rasp, comb,
silver sand, hessian or open-
weave fabric, etc.*
sieve†
paint and solvent
dry powder colors
rabbitskin size
best gilder's whiting
acrylic gesso**

matt medium††
knotting

* The materials for texturing are suggestions only, as explained in Method.
† Use the sieve to mix the whiting into the size, but only sieve once as this can introduce air bubbles into the water.
** Acrylic gesso is a readymade gesso as an alternative to making your own, but it does not have the same range of uses.
†† Matt medium is a dilutant for acrylic gesso, obtainable from the same supplier as the gesso.

---

*1* To apply a priming coat to the raw wood, take a little gesso and melt it in a double boiler. Add 25 per cent water to thin it, and when the mix is very hot, brush it onto the wood using a hogshair brush. The hot size will soak into the wood, giving a good key for subsequent coats of undiluted gesso.

*2* Allow at least 24 hours for the wood to swell and settle down again before applying further gesso.

*3* Apply the following coats, with the gesso lukewarm, in quite quick succession, not allowing them to dry completely between applications so that all the coats join together as a solid mass. You will get better adhesion and more even coverage of you stipple each coat rather than brushing it; but lay a smooth coat as a last layer.

*4* The number of coats you need to apply depends on the purpose of the gesso. As a ground for water gilding you need an average of eight coats because the surface must be absolutely smooth, with no trace of the wood grain beneath. If the molding is to be heavily decorated with paints and varnishes, the grain merely needs to be filled. In this case two coats of gesso will suffice. After sandpapering these two coats, the wood will show through; but the surface will be smooth, and that is what matters.

### Textures

The last coat of gesso can be used to make a texture. Take a small stretch at a time, and coat up. While the gesso is still wet, textures can be created in many different ways, including the following:

– Stippling, using a stiff brush;

– Combing across the width of the molding, using a plastic or metal comb;
– Laying hessian or other open-weave fabric onto the surface. Either press the hessian into the surface, and then remove; or leave the fabric in place and apply another coat of gesso on top;
– Sprinkling silver sand onto the surface.

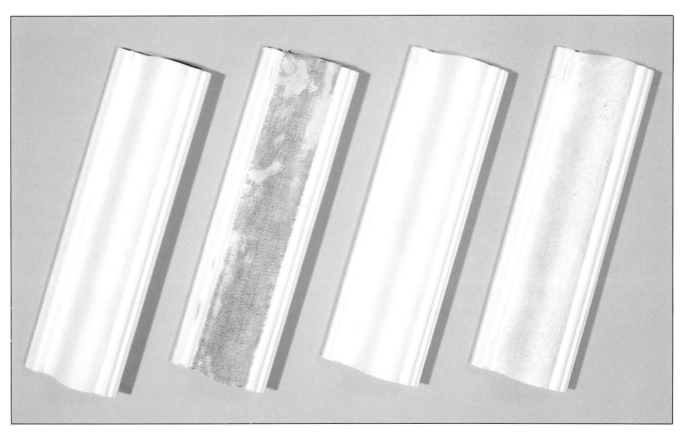

*Examples of textured gesso effects – from left to right: adding dry pigment; adding hessian; combing; sprinkling silver sand.*

### Finishes Over Gesso

A heavily-textured surface lends itself wonderfully to a painted finish; glazes can be laid on and left in the crevices to create a rich, patinated surface. If a smooth surface is wanted, you can sandpaper the last coat with 320-grit silicone carbide sandpaper. Wipe the sanded surface with a clean cotton rag dipped in cold water. This will not only smooth the surface: you will find that, when the gesso dries, it will be harder than before the wetting.

If the gesso is to be painted, it must first be sealed with a mixture consisting of paint and solvent in equal parts. When this is completely dry, full coats of paint can be applied, followed by glazes if required.

Another attractive finish can be achieved with dry powder colors. The method is as follows:

*1* Apply gesso, leaving brushmarks on the last coat.

*2* When dry, dust the surface with french chalk to make it slippery and smooth.

*3* Apply dry powder color with a soft shaving brush or cottonwool.

*4* Sandpaper the surface.

*5* Seal the surface with wax furniture polish.

### Carving

A heavy coating of gesso can be carved. The surface can either be worked dry or it can be dampened with cold water to soften it. Wood carving tools and traditional carving techniques can be used. Alternatively, for those who wish to develop this art, there is a range of special tools with different shaped heads, called "gesso hooks" (obtainable from gilding suppliers).

### Acrylic Gesso

If you do not wish to mix your own gesso, you can buy acrylic gesso, a readymade commercial form, and use it as a base for painting the frame.

Check the raw timber for smoothness, and if necessary smooth the wood with 320-grit sandpaper. Seal any knots with knotting to prevent resin coming through and spoiling your finish. Fill any holes with wood stopping, and sandpaper smooth when dry.

Dilute the first coat of acrylic gesso with an equal part of matt medium. Subsequent coats can be applied straight from the pot. When the second coat has thoroughly dried, wet-sand the surface using 800 wet-or-dry sandpaper to achieve a beautifully smooth, marble-like finish. Two coats should be sufficient to prepare the surface for painting.

# GILDING

$G$old has been used to decorate moldings ever since the frame, as a separate entity from the picture, evolved during the Italian Renaissance.

As a sympathetic and flattering surrounding to a painting or mirror that will blend with any background, gold with its shimmering reflective surface is perfect from every point of view. In candle-lit interiors, gold surfaces flicker and shine, endowing a room with a rich warmth and beauty. The surface needs little cleaning other than dusting, and in time the gold, far from tarnishing as other metals do, increases in splendor. Many hobbyists are wary of gilding, believing it to be not only expensive but difficult to apply. In fact, its beauty and durability far outweigh any disadvantages and it is well worth learning how to do it.

Gilding involves the application of gold leaf to the surface of the frame. There are two kinds of gilding for frames: water gilding and oil gilding. Gold leaf needs to adhere to the surface, and the method of adhesion is either a *water*-based glue or a linseed-based *oil* size.

Silver leaf can be used in the same ways, but it must be lacquered to prevent tarnishing.

## WATER GILDING

This is the very best of gilding, used for the finest frames. In order to achieve a contrast between matt and burnish, which is the great beauty of gilding of all kinds, a high burnish is needed. This is possible to create on a wooden molding only by thorough treatment of the surface with gesso and bole (a preparation made from clay) prior to laying the leaf. Being skilled-labor-intensive, this work adds to the cost, thus creating the water gilding's reputation for great expense.

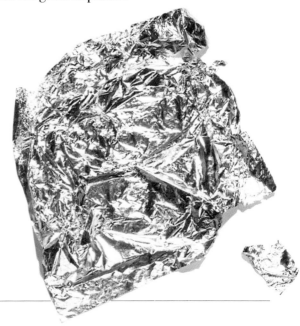

**Materials**

rabbitskin glue and whiting for gesso*
sandpaper
yellow and red bole
hessian or stiff brush
gold leaf
gilder's cutch or cushion
gilder's knife
gilder's tip
agate burnisher
weak size†

pumice powder and felt or very fine wool

* The mixing of gesso is described on page 86.
† The size is the same mixture as used for making gesso, but further diluted by adding 5 parts water to 1 of size. To test, place in the refrigerator; it should *just* set to a soft jelly.

*4* Pick up the gold with a specially designed brush called a tip, and, with the tip and gold in one hand, wet the surface of the molding with cold water and immediately lay the gold onto the surface. The water soaks into the bole-treated surface, drawing the gold down with it. A little size in the water helps adhesion. When the gold is firmly laid and the molding surface beneath is dry, the first burnish can be carried out, using an agate burnisher. Work gently first in one direction then in another. Apply more pressure until a fine deep burnish is achieved. The matt areas can be coated with one or two layers of weak size to protect the gold.

*1* Coat the surface of the molding with up to eight layers of gesso (*see page 86*). Allow to dry, then rub smooth with sandpaper.

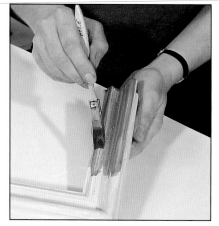

*2* Seal the gesso with yellow bole, which is made from clay mixed with a weak solution of rabbitskin glue.

*3* Apply one coat of yellow bole, rub smooth with a brush or piece of hessian, then follow with three or four progressively weaker coats of red bole. If the molding is deeply carved, apply the red bole only to the tops of carvings and moldings. This is because, if you fail to gild the depths, the molding will not shriek red, but rather show the more sympathetic yellow bole color. When these layers of bole are dry, sandpaper

or brush the surface until very smooth, and gilding can begin.

The gold used in water gilding is not attached to a tissue backing. And, because the gold is so thin, it cannot be handled with fingers – it would stick to them and disintegrate. Various tools have been devised to handle the gold, notably the gilder's cutch, or cushion. This is a leather-covered pad with a shield of parchment at one end. Several sheets of gold are tipped into the back of the cutch, and the gilder brings forward one leaf at a time to cut to size and lay.

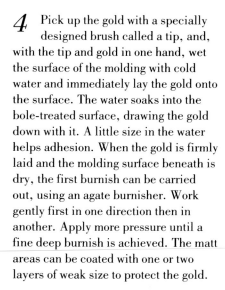

*Left: Gold leafed frame with combed finish. Center: Florentine-style frame
finished with gold leaf. Right: Dutch metal leafed frame.*

## Antiquing

The aging process for water gilding usually involves distressing – that is, removing gold rather than applying layers of dirt. A gentle rub over the burnished or protected area with pumice powder and felt, or *very* fine steel wool, will wear through the gold, revealing the fine overlaps of leaf so characteristic of old gilding. These overlaps are recognized as a mark of fine gilding and are widely imitated by a variety of methods. The rubbing will also reveal a little of the bole undercoat.

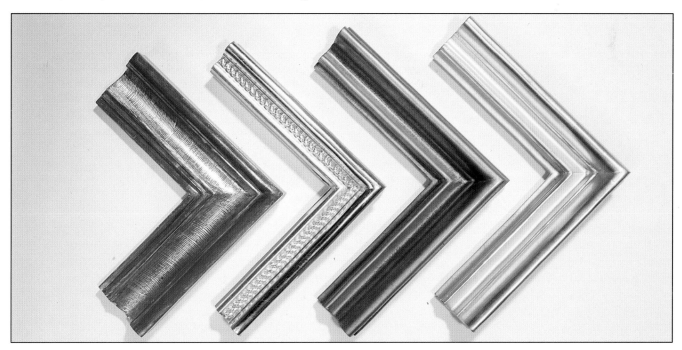

*Different types of gilding – from left to right: combed Dutch metal leaf; bright
gold leaf with rope pattern; bronze powder dusted onto gold size; solid gold finish
with bright gold leaf.*

## OIL GILDING

This is a cheaper and quicker method of gilding and it is suitable for any clean, non-porous surface, including metal and stone. It is also the only kind of gilding used for exterior work. It cannot be burnished. On picture frames it can be used to great effect in combination with paint to pick out ornament and detail.

Transfer gold leaf is used. Each sheet is backed with paper which makes it easier to handle.

Working to the highest standards, aim to make the gilded surface as similar as possible to the appearance of the gold in the book: the condition of the surface of the molding and application of the adhesive should change the character and appearance of the gold as little as possible. For the very best results in oil gilding, the ideal surface is one that has been sprayed with cellulose paint (*see page 76*). The surface is as smooth as plastic – and the gold looks smooth and bright. It would be very unusual to achieve such a finish on a hand-painted surface, and it is unlikely that such a gloss will be required, but at least it *can* be achieved if it is wanted.

The surface of the molding should be prepared with an oil-based size. There is a variety of these sizes to choose from. They vary in drying time, and generally the size that takes the longest to dry will give the best results. If possible, use 24-hour size or, if unobtainable, 12-hour.

Proceed as follows:

---

**Materials**

oil-based size
book of transfer gold leaf
stiff brushes
scissors for cutting gold
ormolu thinned with an equal part of denatured alcohol (methylated spirits), for protection and to even the finish

---

*1* Lay the size on the prepared surface as thinly as possible with a stiff brush.

*2* Take another brush, and in smooth, even strokes remove the size, wiping the brush on a clean rag between strokes.

This thin coat of size will, over the next twelve or so hours, find its own level, so that the layer of glue on which to sit the gold is as even as possible. (If a quicker-drying size is used, it has insufficient time to level out, and the resultant ridges and unevenness in the adhesive will dull the gold.) Although the size is called "12-hour," you will probably find that the drying time will extend to 18 hours. Test the readiness of the size by pulling your knuckle along the surface, preferably at the side of the molding. You should hear a high pitched squeak if the size is ready. Alternatively, try the hairs on the back of your hand; they should *just* stick to the size.

*3* Now take the book of transfer gold. Each leaf is about 3¼ in (82 mm) square. If you are gilding a narrow molding, cut strips of leaf slightly wider than the molding. You can cut the whole book up all at once if you need that much – so if the molding is ½ in (13 mm) wide, cut the whole book through into six equal divisions.

*4* Lay one strip at a time over the size. Press firmly with your fingers and the backing will come away, leaving the gold in place. Carry on around the frame, pushing the gold from behind the tissue into awkward corners with an old, worn-down hogshair brush or similar tool.

*5* Finally, you may wish to apply a protective coat of ormolu to the gold. This is a pale yellow alcohol-based lacquer, which is thinned half and half with denatured alcohol (methylated spirits). Apply it to the gold with a dryish brush.

*Examples of composition ornaments made from carved wooden molds and finished with gold leaf.*

## POWDER GILDING

This is a much more economical method of gilding. The finish it produces is never as bright as gold leaf, and the surface needs to be sealed as it will tarnish.

The color range of metallic powders is very wide; the quality varies, too, from very fine to coarse.

These powders can either be bound into a medium and then painted on, or they can be dusted onto a sticky surface. The disadvantage of the latter method is that the powder is very light and tends to get everywhere, which is wasteful – and it is not easy to dislodge.

---

*Materials*

metallic powders
shellac, or Japan oil size
mineral spirits (white spirit) for cleaning brushes, splashes, etc.
cotton velvet
materials for antiquing: oil color*, colored wax*, pigment, wood ash, dirt
soft cloth
polyurethane varnish or ormolu to lacquer

* Use earthy colors to tone down the gold, such as umber, sienna, earth green. Keep the coloring cool; avoid hot colors. Wax can be mixed with pigments (in the same color range) or can be bought ready stained.

---

*1* You can bind the powder and use it as a paint by mixing it into shellac, or Japan oil size (the latter needs to be diluted with an equal part of mineral spirits/white spirit).

*2* The powder is best dusted on by applying it onto a slow-drying oil size, as in oil gilding. If you are in a

hurry, lay Japan size as thinly as possible and, when it is nearly dry, dust the powder onto that. To apply the powder, transfer it from a dish to the surface with a folded piece of cotton velvet. Whichever method of application is used, allow the surface to dry completely, then apply a thin coat of varnish overall to protect it.

*3* For an antiqued effect, this last coat can be tinted, if required, with oil color to tone down the gold; then, when that is dry, a colored wax can be applied. Before the wax has hardened, dust a mixture of pigment, wood-ash, and general dirt into the corners, and then buff up overall with a soft cloth. Only a very light application of dirt is necessary: it is easy to overdo the aging process, so be circumspect.

# THE
# FRAME

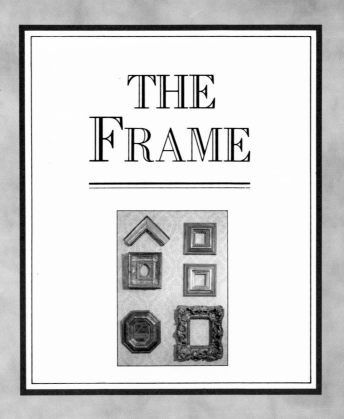

# THE FRAME

*T*o the outsider a picture frame may seem to be a very simple thing: four pieces of molding fastened at the corners. In fact, of course, frames come in an infinite variety of materials, sizes, and shapes.

The picture framer's first step after selecting the molding for a particular subject is to cut the miters to the correct rabbet (rebate) size. The rabbet (rebate) is the stepped or grooved section into which the glass will fit when the picture and frame are assembled. Thus the length of each miter is equal to the corresponding side of the glass, plus about $\frac{1}{16}$ in or a couple of millimeters to allow for clearance.

It does not matter how the miters are cut, as long as they are near perfect. Miters may look good when two corners are offered together, but unless

they are as near perfect as makes no difference, gaps will begin to show when the whole frame is assembled.

If you are a beginner, you would be well advised to put plenty of practice into this the most basic of framing techniques. Whether you are working with a chopper or an electric saw, learn how to adjust your particular make of machine to achieve the best results. Learn how to recognize the awkward moldings, such as those that tend to chip in the composition when cut or produce an uneven back, or aluminum moldings as described below, and avoid them in the future. There are many other aspects of technique you will learn – or even develop yourself – only as a result of experience. But there are a few practical hints that can be mentioned here and now.

# USING A MITER BOX

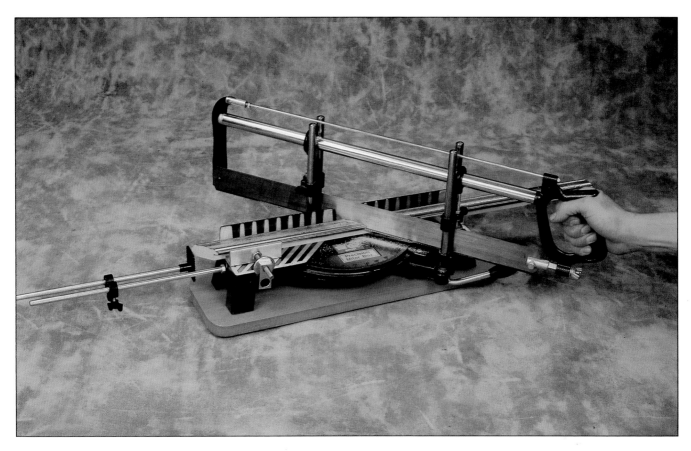

Miters can be cut in moldings using a tenon saw and a simple metal miter vise, or one of the types of miter block (*see page 27*). The miter vise can also be used as a corner clamp (*see page 100*).

First you need to establish the dimensions of the frame. Measure the length and width of the canvas

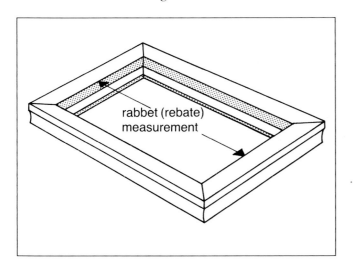

rabbet (rebate) measurement

or the mat (mount) board area. When transferring these measurements to the molding, you need to measure from the "rabbet" or "rebate", i.e. the stepped edge on the inside of the molding, as shown in the diagram. The top edge of the molding is called the "sight" edge and this is the edge which overlaps the image.

When cutting molding, get into the habit of cutting the longest lengths first. If you make any mistakes with them, they can be used to make the short sides. Offer the first cut piece to the other assembled components, such as glass, mat (mount), and back, to make sure that it has been cut big enough; any adjustments can be made at this point. Always allow a little bit extra; it is easy to cut molding down to size.

If using a plastic miter block, place a thin strip of wood between the molding and the plastic, to protect the base.

# USING MITER CUTTERS

*B*oth electric saws and choppers have at least one thing in common: the method of setting for cutting the length of molding required.

### Calibration

Nearly all machinery is now calibrated in metric units, though some manufacturers offer the option of imperial calibration.

The present style of calibration consists of three scales: one for measuring the width to be cut (that is, from the back of the molding to the edge of the rabbet/rebate); one for the required length of the piece of molding; and a stop to set this length at the required molding width. For example, for a

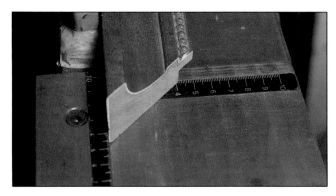

molding length of 12 in (300 mm) and a molding base width of 5⅝ in (41 mm), set the cutting stop at 300 on the engraved scale on the V-support arm for a metric machine and 41 on the scale on the cutting stop (*see photographs above and below*).

After trimming the first miter, you can make the setting for the first two pieces of molding for the frame, assuming that you are making only one frame. Always cut the longer pieces first, so that if you make a mistake on those, you can use them for the shorter sides.

As mentioned above, when using a chopper, several "bites" need to be taken on the wider

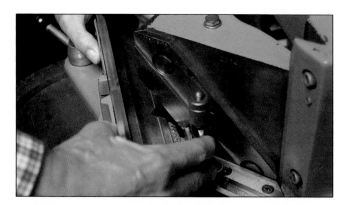

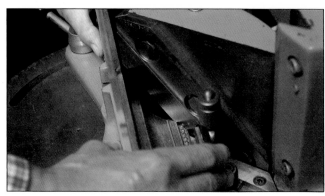

moldings as shown in the three photographs (*left*). It may seem obvious advice, but get into the habit of checking the first cut length of molding against the subject to be framed. You will avoid wasting a considerable length of molding if you satisfy yourself at this stage that no last minute adjustments need to be made. Incidentally, it is always worth checking your pile of molding off-cuts before starting with a fresh length of molding: it is probably the only way they will ever get used! Always keep a check, too, on the rabbet (rebate) supports. These are the devices on a chopper that prevent the rabbet (rebate) overhang from being crushed. (A saw does not need them as its cutting motion is circular rather than vertical.) Slight variations in rabbet (rebate) depth on moldings may affect the accurate cutting of every piece. This can become important if you are cutting a large number of pieces.

Take great care when setting the rabbet (rebate) supports. If you set them too high, the miters will never come together properly at the top. If you set them too low, the molding will tip inward under pressure and form a gap at the back.

To set the supports correctly, hold the molding against the back support and apply firm downward pressure to ensure the base is properly in contact with the bed. Now carefully move in the cutting head, then bring in the supports and adjust them so that you can feel resistance when they are raised underneath the rabbet (rebate). If you are cutting a long run of a particular molding set the lock-nut in place so that the supports do not move. If you are cutting a selection of different moldings, you will have to re-set the supports for each.

Care and attention to detail always pay dividends on this operation. It is better to take a little more time to cut the molding accurately rather than rushing to complete the job. Prepare all the constituent parts, before assembling the frame.

### Problem Moldings

When cutting some of those moldings that have a thin aluminum covering, you may find it difficult to make a clean cut at the back of the molding; the aluminum covering is inclined to tear, producing an ugly appearance at the corner. This is due to the action of the chopper blades, which press the metal skin downward rather than cutting it. It happens because the blades are unable to penetrate far enough to the back of the molding to allow the blade edges to do their work.

The cure is to thrust the molding further in toward the blades, so that a larger area of cutting edge can get to work. The best way to do this is by

sticking two strips of mat (mount) board, about 1 in (25 mm) deep, onto the back support (or beating bar) and holding the molding against them (*see photograph*). This has the effect of moving the molding $\frac{1}{12}$ in (2 mm) further under the blades. Be sure to make your reading for setting the molding *after* you have made this modification.

Another problem may occur with aluminum-covered moldings on a core or base-wood that is too soft. The crushing action of the chopper blades presses the aluminum skin into the core, resulting in severe denting at the corners. The best way to avoid this is simply to buy better-quality moldings in the first place. But if you have bought an inferior product, and if the molding has a perfectly flat top, you can prevent denting by simply turning the molding upside-down, so that the aluminum "skin" is underneath the wood core. The settings remain the same, but you do not need the rabbet (rebate) supports.

Remember, however, that this works only with perfectly flat-topped aluminum-covered moldings. Circular saws generally cut this type of molding rather better than a chopper. But even saws can have problems with "snatching" of the blade on the final section of the cut.

# PUTTING THE FRAME TOGETHER

## USING THE MITER VISE

When the molding has been cut, move over to the assembly bench to put the frame together. If you do not have an underpinner, the mitering vise is the next stop. Establish a method of working and always arrange the pieces to be fastened together in the same way on the bench. I always use the formula "long-left", so that I never get the pieces mixed up and find myself with two corners that don't go together.

A typical vise consists essentially of two screw-driven clamps mounted at right angles on a cast-iron base. Although most vises come mounted on a swiveling and tilting turret, the most effective way to use the tool is to separate the top from its turret base and mount it in a corner of the workbench with its top surface flush with the bench top. You need to make sure that the operating

wheels for the clamps are not obstructed.

Position the two pieces of molding in the clamps, line up the miters, then clamp securely. Next, remove one of the pieces and apply the adhesive. Almost all proprietary wood glue sold today is white polyvinyl acetate (PVA). If an extra strong bond is required, or if the wood is so soft that it absorbs too much of the glue, apply a thin glaze of water-diluted glue first to seal the miters of both pieces and allow it to dry. Then apply the full-strength glue in the normal way. Replace in the clamp. Do the same with the second piece of molding.

Remove any excess glue that may have seeped out at this point. I find a ½in (13 mm) paintbrush, slightly dampened, is very useful for this, particularly on heavily decorated profiles.

The corners now need to be fastened. This is done with pins whose length and thickness are determined by the width of the molding; they range from veneer pins for the smaller profiles, up to 16-gauge panel pins for the larger ones. A pin hammer is best for driving the nails home – a ¼ lb (113 g) one for the veneer pins and perhaps double that weight for the larger pins.

Always drill pilot holes for the pins. If you try to hammer them directly into the molding you will almost certainly split it. A small joiner's wheeled drill is best for this job (an electric drill is too cumbersome). Don't be tempted to use fine wood drill bits: they are very fragile and quite expensive. Nip the head off one of the pins that you are using,

put this in the chuck, and drill the holes with it. It works perfectly satisfactorily – and you have a plentiful supply of them. They also have the great advantage of being exactly the right size.

Some of the harder timbers are very difficult to penetrate, causing the pins to bend at a critical point and involving irritating and fiddly extraction. If you dip the tip of the pin into the oil before use, you will find this makes life much easier. Space out the pins according to the height and width of the molding, and stagger them so that they don't line up with one another; this removes any remaining danger of splitting.

Keep the pilot holes as horizontal as possible to avoid any possibility of the pin penetrating the base or, even worse, the top of the molding. Hammer the pin in until it is not quite flush with the molding side; then drive it below the surface with a nail driver or punch.

The resultant hole now needs filling with one of the proprietary brands of colored nail-hole and corner fillers. Give the corner of the miter a quick dressing with fine sandpaper to remove any rough edges, and smear some of the filler around the corner so as to color any pale wood which may be showing. Finally, wipe off excess filler.

Assemble two Ls before completing the frame.

## — USING THE UNDERPINNER —

When using an underpinner, first of all check that you have the correct wedges in the magazine. The size you require is governed by the depth of the molding – but as only three sizes of wedge are available, this will not take you long. The wedge will need to have at least $\frac{1}{12}$ in (2 mm) of timber above it to avoid any risk of splitting. Because some moldings are quite deep, it may be necessary to "stack" wedges, one on top of another. You fire a second wedge immediately after the first, which is consequently driven farther into the molding; in effect, you have a wedge of double depth.

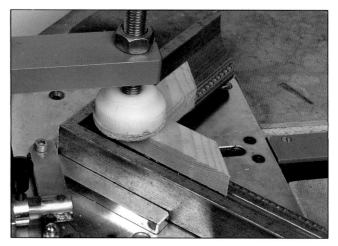

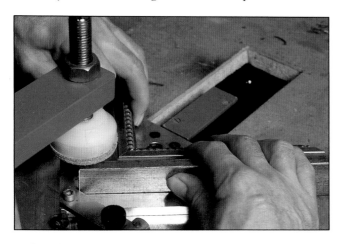

Set the machine so that the wedges are fired exactly into the desired position. This is largely determined by the shape of the molding's profile. Relatively flat moldings are the easiest since they are of the same shape right across the width, but some profiles are very intricately shaped.

The thing to remember is that the wedge, when driven in, must have counteracting support directly above it. With many complicated profiles this is not always possible, so you will need to prepare a few pieces of packing to compensate for any differences in relative depths, because the top clamp of the machine will press only on the highest point of the molding. You can make up these pieces of packing from varying thicknesses of timber by cutting a right-angle "L" shape and lining the underneath with cork or felt to act as a cushion.

Unless you are absolutely familiar with the particular molding you are using, always start by cutting two small practice pieces to fasten together; this will show up any peculiarities in performance and allow you to make necessary adjustments. Check that the pressure of the clamps, for instance, is just right. If it is too great, there is a danger of crushing the molding; if it is too little, the wedge will not be driven home fully and the molding will lift when the machine is operated.

The distance of travel of the stroke on an underpinner is generally about 1 in (25 mm); bear this in mind when setting the top clamp in relation to the molding. In other words, the driver, which strips a wedge from the magazine and pushes it upward, works in opposition to the top clamp which needs to travel downward for the same distance before it completes its operating stroke. This applies to both manual and pneumatic machines, except that on some of the more sophisticated models the holding clamp is pressure-sensitive, so that the top clamp requires no adjustment.

Once you have established that the underpinner is operating correctly and that you have set it to suit the particular molding that you are using, you can begin to assemble the frame. The easiest way to work is to assemble two halves of the frame first and then to complete the frame by fastening these two together. You should try to get two wedges into the frame at each corner, unless the molding is of very small section, in which case one will suffice; on some wider moldings more than two may be required. The two main wedges are the inner and outer ones and more often than not are all that are

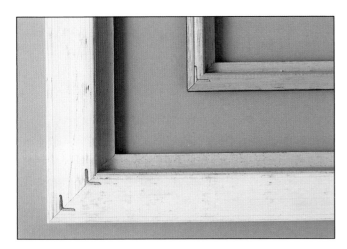

needed. In any case, the depth of the wedge is more important than the number used. Moreover, the combination of wedges and glue is much more effective than either of these methods by itself.

The ideal set-up is to have an underpinner in one corner of the island work-bench and a miter vise in the other: I frequently come across moldings that for one reason or another simply do not like underpinners. The miter vise, although a lot slower, is perhaps surer.

When making a frame using aluminum-covered molding, you will find that the pin heads dent the surrounding aluminum skin, making for an ugly finish. You can't use a filler because it will not adhere to the metal surface. The only practical solution is to arrange the nailing so that the pins finish on the top and bottom edges of the frame,

thus removing them at least partly from sight.

For those jobs where it is unnecessary to use nail-hole filler (as when using an underpinner) but you still need to dress up the corners of the frame, it is worth equipping yourself with a battery of felt-tipped pens in a range of shades to match the colors of different moldings. A quick touch-up with one of these will save messing around with brushes and woodstains.

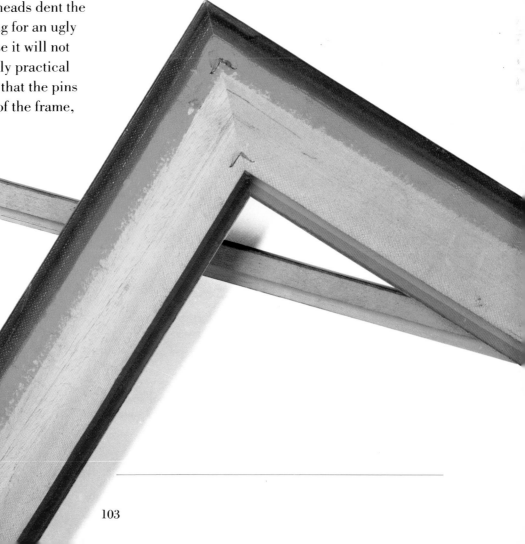

# FINAL ASSEMBLY

With the frame complete, you can now assemble all the components. Carry out these various operations on a sheet of light-colored mat (mount) board stapled to the bench and replaced regularly. Let us assume your subject is a print.

### Backing board

The choice of board is determined by price, weight, rigidity and whether or not it is acid-free.

The most commonly-used material for the backing board is hardboard or masonite in $\frac{1}{12}$ in (2 mm) thickness. Easily cut with a craft knife or guillotine, it has an acceptable rigidity with minimal thickness. Its disadvantages are its hydroscopic nature and its weight.

The next most popular board is greyboard which comes in varying thicknesses. It cuts easily with a craft knife or guillotine but has a comparatively inferior rigidity.

Corrugated board is an extremely effective backing board because of its good rigidity to weight ratio. It also compares well in price with the previous two types and there is a new blue acid-free corrugated board now available. It can be cut with either craft knife or guillotine.

Foam-core is expensive but it has maximum rigidity with minimum weight and a reasonable thickness. It is easy to cut with a craft knife. (A guillotine cannot be used.)

---

**Materials**

print
mat (mount), cut to shape
backing board, cut to shape
glass, cut to shape
glass cleaner*
lint-free cloth
glazing gun and darts
sealing tape†
slim craft knife

\* See page 67 for details of a homemade glass cleaner.
† Choose a width of sealing tape to suit the frame: see step 10.

---

*1* Place the print face down on the bench and stick two strips of adhesive tape at its top corners in such

a way that half of each strip sticks to the print and half is free to stick to the underside of the mat (mount).

*2* Turn the print over (face up) and place the mat (mount) over the subject, taking great care to align the bevels with any edges that will be visible on the mounted print.

*3* Press the top corners of the mat (mount) into place at the points where the tape has been attached to the print. This will keep the mat (mount) aligned with the print and requires no further alteration. Place this onto the backing board, which is cut to the same dimensions as the glass.

*4* Thoroughly clean both sides of your glass with glass cleaner and a lint-free cloth, paying particular attention to the edges. Buff lightly with a clean cloth and check for any specks of dust.

*5* Support the mat (mount)/print/ backing board sandwich underneath with one hand, and lift the edge of the glass with the other.

*6* Slip the sandwich under the glass and lower it gently into position. Align the glass/mat (mount), etc. carefully at the edges and make a final check for dirt specks. If any have to be removed, lift the edge of the glass closest to you very slowly (so as not to create the sucking effect of a vacuum) and carefully remove the offending particles.

*7* Lay the frame in place over the subject.

*8* Lift the whole assembly with both hands, and turn it over so that the frame is now face down on the bench with the package of components neatly inside.

*9* Take your glazing gun and fasten the components into the frame, spacing the darts evenly about every 4 in (100 mm). Place the outside of the frame against a substantial weight to

give the glazing gun some resistance to fire against, otherwise lighter-weight moldings will begin to bow away from the backing. When using the gun, apply even pressure downward onto the backing to ensure the glass is tight against the rabbet (rebate) of the molding. It is good practice to fasten the subject initially with just the minimum quantity of darts necessary to hold it in the frame, and then to raise the frame on one edge and check finally for dust specks.

*10* When all the darts have been fitted, seal around the rabbet (rebate) with tape. Make sure the tape is aligned parallel with the edge of the frame, and stretch it very lightly so that there is no danger of any wrinkles.

If the molding rabbet (rebate) is deep enough to allow the glass/mat (mount)/backing sandwich to be sunk below the level of the frame base, first buff the tape into place on the molding only, then slice through the tape at either end against the right-angle formed by the sides of the frame. Run a rag firmly along the inner edge of the molding, working from the center outward, forcing the tape down into the corners of the frame and backing.

Use a width of tape appropriate to the size of the frame, unless you are covering the back of the frame with Kraft paper. This is a method to use on extra-special pieces of work. The idea is that the back presents a flat brown surface that is completely dust-sealed. The method is as follows:

*1* Tape the back of the frame in the normal way.

*2* Cut a piece of Kraft (brown) paper slightly bigger than the frame, place it shiny side down on the bench, and thoroughly dampen the dull side of the paper with a wet sponge.

*3* Place the frame face down on the bench and brush PVA builder's adhesive all around the base of the molding, avoiding getting any on the backing.

*4* Take the dampened brown paper and stretch it over the back of the frame, pressing it into place with a rag.

*5* Using a straight edge, trim the excess paper away about ⅛ in (3 mm) in from the edge of the frame.

*6* Remove any excess glue and leave to dry.

The paper will have expanded when it was dampened. As it dries it will shrink and become drum-tight across the back, provided it has been stuck down securely.

*Corner samples displaying a variety of shiny, matt and colored finishes for
aluminum moldings.*

# VARIATIONS ON A THEME

*I*n this chapter we have dealt with the most basic framing procedures and materials. We finish it with a brief look at some variations.

Picture framers are today making increasing use of extruded aluminum section. For many years the aluminum frame was hindered by the limited number and variety of profiles available; most such frames simply provided a variation on the basic cushion, or "hockeystick," variety (*see page 74*). Recently, however, such an enormous variety of new American sections and profiles has become available that almost anything appears to be possible.

Far from providing merely a neat edge around a poster, aluminum profiles up to 2 in (50 mm) in width are now common, and aluminum is even used with canvas stretchers. The finishes, also, have left behind the simple gold and silver polished or satin effects, and beautiful pastel shades and mottled finishes are now available from a multitude of companies.

Aluminum extrusion is used by most framers in its ready-mitered form. Suppliers offer it in stock lengths as well – but remember that you need an electric saw to cut it. It is worth considering whether you need this extra problem, particularly in view of the fact that the "chop" (mitering) service is so efficient now.

Perhaps the greatest advantage of the aluminum frame is its strength in relation to the size of its profile, which puts it at the top of the shopping list when considering molding for the large, modern poster-type prints, when all that is required is a neat, slender edge to contain the subject. Many different depths of profile are available, and they now rival timber moldings in the thicknesses of work that they can accommodate. Ease of assembly is also a very large plus point, the only tool needed being a screwdriver.

Measure the work accurately when using aluminum – the chop service supplier will make the necessary clearance allowances. Remember to trim the corners on the finished frame with a smooth file; otherwise the sharp edges can give you a nasty scratch.

The work contained in an aluminum frame is held tight against the glass by curved spring clips that fit under the back edge of the extrusion. The suppliers never seem to enclose enough of these in the packs of hardware that come with the mitered pieces, so order an extra supply of these; you need one of these clips about every 6 in (150 mm) to be confident of a job well done. Most metal frame kits also come with small self-adhesive squares of soft plastic to stick to the corners of the frame when it has been assembled. Use them – they will prevent the back of the frame tearing the wallpaper.

Handle the lengths of frame very carefully and keep them wrapped in the tissue they arrive in until you need them: it is important to keep them in prime condition, as a scratch on aluminum cannot be disguised with a spot of wood-stain.

# BOX FRAMES

*A*nother common framing requirement is to accommodate thick subjects, such as lino-blocks or carved wooden items. These will need what is known as a box-frame. This is exactly what it says it is: a box within a frame. It can be constructed from simple rectangular-section timber of appropriate depth, with a plywood or hardboard base and covered with a suitable material. The main problem with box frames is that you never seem to be able to get exactly the right depth of timber you need. Also, they involve extra cutting, pinning, and messy assembly. The advent of foam-core board has made many things possible, or simpler, for the framer, and box-frames are one of them. To construct a strong box-frame, first measure the size of base required. Add to this on all four sides the depth of the sides of the box. Now proceed as follows:

**Materials**

foam-core board
measure
straight mat (mount) cutter
general adhesive
adhesive tape
craft knife
display velvet
panel adhesive

*1* Cut out a blank of this size in ³⁄₁₆ in (5 mm) foam core. This thickness is ideal, but ⅛ in (3 mm) will also work well. Anything thicker tends to produce a clumsy result.

*2* Mark the depths of the sides on the reverse of the foam-core, extending the lines to the edges, so that the corner area is clearly delineated.

*3* In the corner area, mark a line ³⁄₁₆ in (5 mm), i.e. the thickness of the foam-core, in from the lines already drawn, on one side of each corner only.

*4* To cover the interior of the box, cut the material (display velvet is ideal) large enough to overlap the foam core blank by about 1 in (25 mm) on all

sides. Glue this to the right side of the foam-core blank, leaving the overlapping pieces free.

*5* Turn the foam-core wrong side up, so that the pencil marks are visible. Using a craft knife with a new blade, cut out the corner pieces being careful to follow the second line marking the thickness of the foam-core, as made in step 3.

*6* On the remaining lines, which mark the base area of the box, cut through the *surface of the foam core only*.

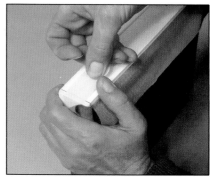

*7* Fold up the sides of the box and tape neatly in position. The extra section at each corner serves to line up the corners vertically and gives added strength at these points.

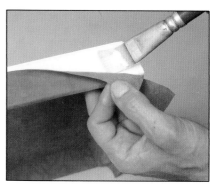

*8* Wrap the excess covering material over the edges of the box and glue in place.

frame may present problems, but applying a bead of panel adhesive (the stuff decorators use to stick mock wood paneling to walls and doors) all around where the box joins the frame and allowing it to set will usually suffice. Fixing hanging anchorages on box frames can also be a problem unless it is thought through beforehand. The most effective method is to incorporate them in the skin of the box during its construction.

The result is a light-weight, rigid box with a good top edge to support the glass. Unfortunately, there are few moldings with enough depth of rabbet (rebate) to contain even the most modest box, but neat taping of the finished item will suffice to give an acceptable appearance. Fixing in the

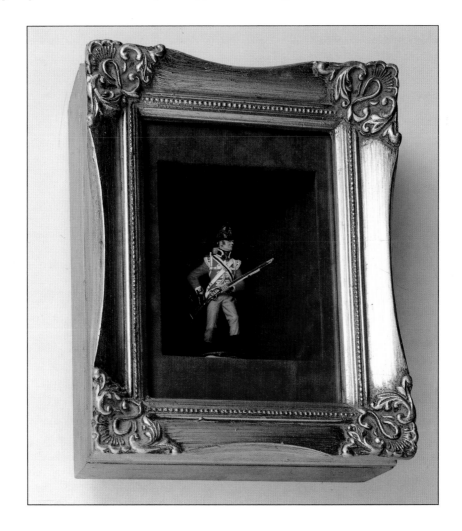

# SHADOW BOXES

*A*nother use of foam-core is in making a shadow box, which is basically a box-frame with a mat (mount). Owing to the use of a mat (mount), the construction of the box does not have to be quite so complicated. Use the foam-core as depth packing under the mat (mount) – in several layers if necessary – until the required depth of spacing is achieved. If the edges of the foam-core are going to show, cover them with tape and use a felt-tipped pen or something similar to color the edges appropriately. Note also that there are a few distributors who stock a very deep-rabbeted (rebated) molding that can substitute for a narrow shadow box.

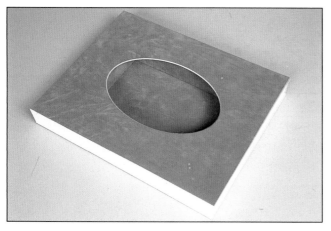

Foam-core can also be used if you wish to frame a valuable bowl or plate. First cover an appropriately-sized piece of mat (mount) board with display velvet. Then cut a circular hole, slightly smaller than the diameter of the subject, in the board with the oval cutter, so that the subject will sit neatly in the hole but cover the edges. Then cut circles of appropriate sizes in foam-core and use these to make the depth underneath. Fix the subject in place using a black outdoor sealant. Then make up the rim-depth of the subject with a ¾ in (19 mm) wide, square-cut mat (mount) covered in suede.

### Adding Interest

Quite often when framing oil-paintings, particularly when they are on board, it seems unsatisfactory simply to throw a bit of molding around it and leave it at that. Apart from the feeling that you have not really achieved much as a framer, the picture usually finishes up looking rather cramped, no matter how fancy the molding may be.

One idea framers rely on to add interest is the use of a double frame, consisting of a small, plain inner frame around the picture itself, an appropriate width of border around that, then a more substantial frame to finish. The space between frames can be filled in with any appropriate material such as hessian or suede.

You can use slip and fillet moldings of all shapes and sizes to add interest to an otherwise humdrum framing job.

### Block Mounting

There is also a process used by framers that uses no molding whatsoever; this is block mounting, which is simply a way of displaying a print in a hangable form in the cheapest, most basic way. You cut a piece of ½in (13 mm) board (either chipboard or the much finer medium-density fiberboard) so that it is ¼in (6 mm) bigger all around than the image area of the print. Form a 45° bevel on the edge of the board halfway down the thickness, and color

the beveled edge black, either with spray paint or brush. Matt black acrylic paint is ideal as it dries quickly and the brush is easily washed out in water.

Much used by gift stores, the block mated (mounted) print is about the most basic that you can get in terms of displaying a print.

### Clip-Frames

One small step up from this is the clip-frame, which consists of a number of clips holding the glass to a backing board, with the subject, and possibly a mat (mount), sandwiched in between. These clips are ingeniously-shaped spring steel arrangements that clip over the edge of the glass while the other end anchors in a recess at a fixed position in the backing board obviating the need for a frame.

### STRUT-BACKS

Photographs are often framed for standing on a horizontal surface such as a mantelpiece or a sideboard. For this you will need what is called a strut-back, which is simply a back with a supporting strut attached. If you decide to make your own strut-backs, you will need to obtain the necessary hardware. These are bars and hinges, consisting of a bar that is attached to the backing board and a hinge that fits on the strut; the hinge clips onto the bar on the backing.

The bar should be fitted to the backing one-third of the way down the completed frame. Measure from the bar to the bottom edge of the molding, add ⅞ in (21 mm), and cut the strut to this length. The strut usually tapers toward the top; its width

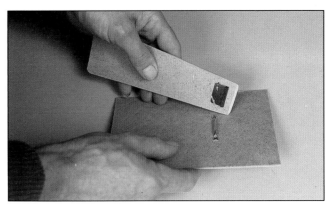

depends on the size of the frame, although strut-back frames rarely exceed 20 × 16 in (500 × 400 mm). The best material to use for making struts is plywood of about ⅙ in (4 mm) thickness.

The bars and hinges are usually attached by bifurcated rivets, but some framers use pop-rivet guns for this. The strut should overhang the bar so that the top of the strut (which should be chamfered on its inner edge) can bear against the back, thus limiting how far the bottom of the strut can be opened. To achieve this, pierce the anchorage holes for the hinge about ⅞ in (21 mm) from the top of the strut.

# DOUBLE-SIDED FRAMES

*O*n occasions, you may need to produce a frame that will display both faces of a double-sided document. The first thing you will need is molding with a rabbet (rebate) up to 1 in (25 mm) deep. To anchor the document effectively you will need a mat (mount) on both sides of the document, and therefore two pieces of glass. The mats (mounts) are cut identically, as are the two pieces of glass. Tape the document neatly in place on the back of one mat (mount) and stick the other mat (mount) to it, back to back, making sure that the mats (mounts) are perfectly aligned. Clean the two pieces of glass and assemble the package. Place the frame over this and turn the whole assembly over. Measure the remaining depth of rabbet (rebate) and cut four strips of backing about ⅛ in (3 mm) thick. Staple the strips around the inside of the rabbet (rebate) to fix the package of

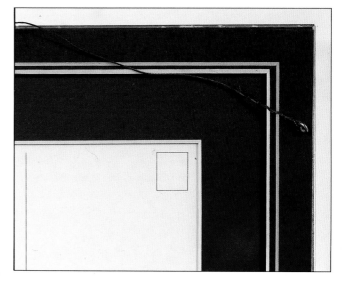

components in place. Finally, color the strips the same shade as the molding. N.B. For documents where conservation is important, there is an acid-free synthetic sheet available.

# FLOATING BOX

Another unusual idea worth knowing about is the "floating" box, in which the subject appears to be suspended in mid-air in the middle of a box-frame. It is made as follows:

*1*  Construct a box from foam-core (*see page 108*), but omit the lining.

*2*  Put in the bottom of the box a base piece of the color and material that the finished interior will be.

*3*  Measure *half* the depth of the box and deduct 1/12 in (2 mm) from that figure.

*4*  Cut four strips of foam-core to this width and cover them with the finishing material.

*5*  Cut these strips to the appropriate length so that they fit around the inside bottom of the box, holding the base piece in place. Ensure that their top edges are covered.

*6*  Cut two pieces of glass to the internal measurement of the top half of the box.

*7*  Lay one piece of glass on the bench and, after cleaning it, fix the subject in place on the glass with double-sided tape. Then clean the other piece of glass and place on top of this, thus holding the subject flat, with edges aligned.

*8*  Place this sandwich in the box so that it rests on the ledge formed by the four covered strips of foam-core.

*9*  Measure the remaining depth in the box, prepare four more strips to this width, and cover them with the finishing material.

*10*  Fasten these in place on top of the glass sandwich, to hold it firmly in place.

*11*  Cut a third piece of glass to sit on top of the box, and frame.

## — VENEERS WITHOUT TEARS —

A product introduced in the United States a few years ago has opened up a wealth of new possibilities for framers and is well worth a mention here. It is basically a wood veneer, and it is manufactured to very fine tolerances, the veneers being of uniform thickness with an even, flat appearance. The sheets of veneer are self-adhesive backed (*see also page 51*).

There are a dozen or so different timber finishes, and they can all be stained and polished as you would expect from a good-quality wood veneer. Its other great attraction is that it is easily cut with a craft knife or even a razor blade. Another unusual virtue of this product is that it folds and bends easily; even a sharp right-angle is no problem.

The adhesive is extremely strong; you must be sure you have the veneer in exactly the right position before pressing it in place – it will not peel off. This product enables mat (mount) board, foam-core, and backing board to be turned into apparently solid timber in an instant. You can use it for making slips for oil paintings, for covering straight and oval mats (mounts), for box frames, and much else.

# DRY MOUNTING/ HEAT SEALING

*L*arge posters or prints that have curled edges or have become misshapen should, if possible, be mounted on a stiffer backing before they are framed. ***Such mounting should never be carried out on original works of art or on items of value***, because the process is not guaranteed irreversible without alteration of the art.

To mount prints by hand, brush on PVA builder's adhesive, which can be reactivated with heat when dry. Be careful not to leave obvious brush marks. Alternatively, for small, quick jobs, spray mount can be used, but it is not as reliable.

If using a dry mounting machine, the procedure is the same for both the hard-bed and the soft-bed types.

It is very important to check the temperature of a press periodically. Under heating fails to activate adhesives truly, over heating exposes the art to temperature extremes that are unnecessary.

*1* Take a piece of dry mounting tissue or film and trim it slightly larger than the subject.

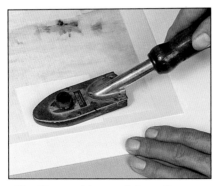

*2* Place the subject face down and, using a tacking iron, tack the tissue in place on the top edge.

*3* Place subject and tissue face up on the mounting substrate and tack in position.

*4* Transfer to the press, close tightly, and leave for the manufacturer's stipulated processing time.

For larger areas it may be necessary to work in sections, in which case an overlap sheet should be used. This is an aluminum sheet which should be approximately 2 in (50 mm) bigger all around than the plate on the press. It has the effect of dissipating pressure at the edge of the platen, thus removing potential marks.

Always use proprietary silicone release paper in immediate contact with the work and change it frequently to prevent residue from one job adversely affecting the next.

The procedure for heat seal laminating is basically the same except that the film covers the subject rather than being underneath it. It gives a protective clear plastic film to the subject. As with dry mounting it should *never* be used on original works of art or items of value.

When placing the film over the subject, keep it wrinkle-free and do not stretch it. Use a thin foam-plastic blanket over the heatseal film to soften the impact of pressure and heat, and to give a pleasing fine texture.

# MULTI-SIDED FRAMES

*I*t's safe to assume that nine out of ten of the picture frames you make will be rectangular or square, but there's no need to confine your activities to these traditional forms. The Victorians, for instance, had a liking for eight-sided frames, especially for mirrors. This shape can be used effectively with oval and circular mats (mounts).

The main problem with multi-sided frames is that, unless the angles are cut absolutely perfectly, the errors have many more chances to compound themselves. The best tool for cutting these angles accurately enough is an electric miter saw with extremely accurate intermediate-angle markings on it and a strong method of locking the cutting head firmly in position. The cheaper machines do not have the finesse to achieve this – so be prepared to

pay quite a lot for a really accurate saw, if you expect to make a large number of this type of frame. (The cutting of other than 45° angles on a mitering guillotine is quite impractical.)

The formula for determining the angle for a multi-sided frame is to divide 180 by however many sides you want. So the angle for a six-sided frame will be 30°, for an eight-sided frame 22.5°, and so on.

If you do not have an underpinner, join the sides of a multi-sided frame using a vise with multi-angle wedge attachments. With underpinners, especially pneumatic machines, the job could not be easier. It is simply a matter of putting the angles together and pressing the pedal. Angle-location plates may be a useful extra – but it is the accuracy of the cut that makes the job easy.

# NEEDLEWORK

Among the less common subjects for framing, tapestries and other pieces of needlework have come to the fore in recent years. The main problem with tapestries is that they have to be stretched – and this can be a laborious chore – so you need to provide a suitably strong substrate on which to do this. If the canvas has been worked on a frame, the distortion will be less. Embroidery books also usually give instructions for stretching a worked piece of canvas, so it is quite likely that the piece to be framed will already have been corrected.

Another problem with tapestries is obtaining moldings in which the rabbets (rebates) are of sufficient depth. The combined thickness of the glass, mat (mount), tapestry, and the thick board over which the tapestry is stretched will probably be about ⅜ in (10 mm) more than most standard moldings will happily contain. So you will be restricted in the range of moldings you can use for

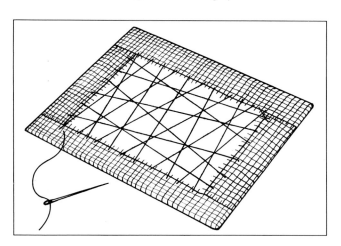

these kinds of subjects.

Ideally, needlework should be laced onto the backing board. Cut the board to the size of the frame. Make sure that the needlework is square, then fold excess fabric to the back and lace to and fro with a strong thread to pull first the right and left sides, then the top and bottom pieces, together (*see diagram*). Alternatively the needlework can be stapled to the backing board, as described below.

If you have to stretch the tapestries yourself, you would be well advised to invest in a tacking gun and rustproof staples, making sure that the gun has double (strong and weak) impact settings, so that you can avoid driving the staples in too far. If you have to frame the subject without a mat (mount), the edge of the material will have to be folded around the edge of the board and secured at the back. As we have seen, the depth of the molding rabbet (rebate) limits the thickness of the board, so you will need to get the shallowest staples possible – no more than ¼ in (6 mm). You will find that ³⁄₁₆ in (5 mm) thick foam-core sandwiched between two pieces of ordinary mat (mount) board makes an ideal base; it is lighter and much easier to cut than plywood.

Foam-core should not be used for very large pieces of needlework, since they can bow over time if they are oversized and the pressure of the supporting fabric is strong.

None of the needleart or silk fibers should come into direct contact with the glass. If the work is to be glazed, a mat (mount) should also be added.

---

*Materials*

tacking gun
rustproof staples
¼ in (6 mm) plywood or foam-
core sandwiched between mat
(mount) board to use as a backboard*

pencil and rule
measure

* Use white or cream board if
framing a pale-colored silk (see
Method).

---

*3* It is simpler to frame tapestries with a mat (mount), and in general the finished work looks better, too. When stretching a tapestry with a mat (mount), cut the base-board oversize to start with, then pencil a line down one side and along the bottom about ½ in (13 mm) greater than the dimensions of the mat (mount).

*1* When starting a stretching operation for close-framing (that is, without a mat/mount) you need to establish what size to cut the board. A good tip is to test the canvas for "stretchability," measuring how far it will pull under medium strain. If you reduce this by ¼ in (6 mm), you will find the dimensions will be just right for wrapping the work around.

*2* Do not skimp with the staples. The gap between them should be no more than one staple-width. Insert the staples at an angle to the weave of the canvas so that each staple applies pressure to as many threads as possible in both weft and warp. It is important when stapling fabric that you are very careful not to tear the fibers with the staples.

*4* Align the equivalent edges of the tapestry with these, and tack it in position at the corners, stretching as you work. Don't apply too much tension, or the stretching will become tighter and tighter as you progress.

*5* After fixing the corners, staple halfway along each side, then halfway between these staples, and so on until all edges are complete.

---

Heavy wool tapestries are by far the trickiest needlework subjects to work with – and unfortunately the most common. Always check for bits of loose wool and other waste material before final assembly of the frame. Silk embroideries are less common, though they seem to be steadily growing in popularity. They are easier to tackle, but a few tips will help you to avoid potential problems.

Never use a tacking gun when stretching silk. The staples might tear the fabric and will create ugly stretch marks right across the material when it is pulled tight. The best method is to stitch the silk to a support fabric (such as flannel) first, then stretch the support as described above.

One thing more to remember when stretching silks: they become even thinner when stretched, so handle with care. For the same reason, always back the silk with white or cream board; it is surprising how much darker the subject can look on even a light shade of plywood.

Finally, it is always worth spending a little extra time on finishing off the backs of framed needlework, especially if it is close-framed. Cover up the exposed edges of the material with an extra board across the backing-board and tape it neatly.

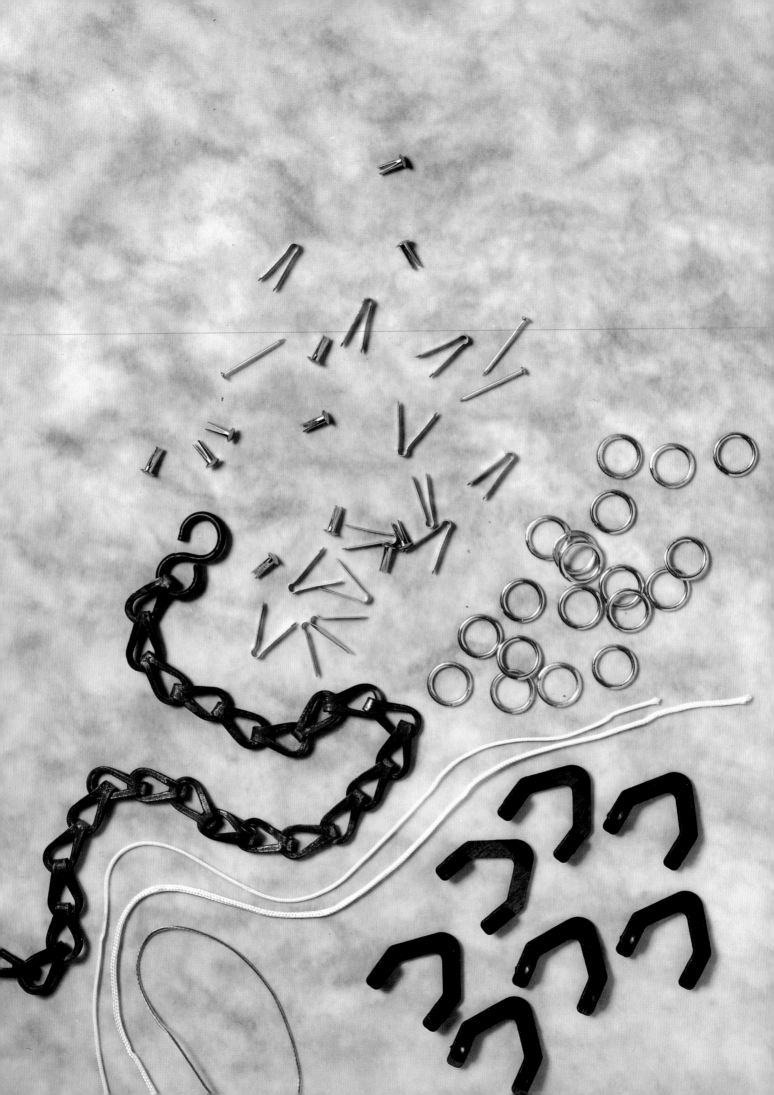

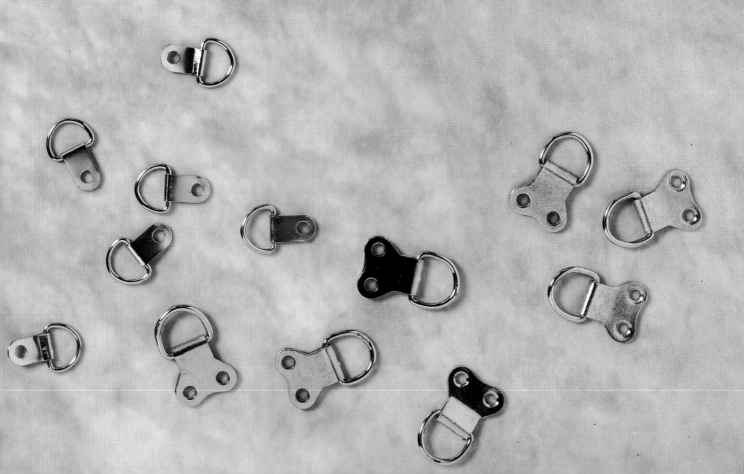

# PICTURE
# HANGING

# HANGING

There must be almost as many methods of hanging frames as there are moldings to choose from. Many are simply variations on a theme, but most are designed for a specific task and so are usually suited only to that one application.

Hanging pictures on walls can never have been more popular than it was in the Victorian age.

The Victorians were very practical about this: they built the method of hanging into the fabric of the building in the form of the picture rail. This tradition was carried through right until the middle of the 20th century, at which time the picture-rail hooks and chains beloved of our grandparents began to disappear in favor of masonry nails and, eventually, the purpose-made picture hook.

You can frame and hang almost anything that takes your fancy. To the dedicated hobbyist, unoccupied wall space is a challenge: even the tiniest area can be filled with a frame containing some special item, be it an oil painting, a print, or perhaps a particularly pretty sea shell.

As a general principle, pictures should be hung to suit their surroundings. For the professional framer, of course, the taste of the customer is paramount, whether he or she simply wants a snapshot of his or her dog framed or he or she has come to place a bulk order for the reception area of some multinational corporation's headquarters. In almost every case, however, the customer is looking for advice and help on style and choice of materials. People react to pictures in different ways. Some are very interested in them and take a lot of notice; for others, they are merely part of the wallcovering.

In public places, pictures represent some part of the interest of strange surroundings, and this should be borne in mind when selecting subjects appropriate to these situations. Never forget the titles of places and people in pictures. If a picture is going to have any extra interest to the onlooker, then the little time spent on titling a subject is surely well spent.

Elizabeth Whiting & Associates

Elizabeth Whiting & Associates

*Botanical pictures grouped round a mirror, pastel prints with white surrounds
on a white wall or an eclectic mixture of square, circular and rectangular
paintings cover the whole surface of the walls, and even the doors. Together they
produce a rich, decorative effect.*

## HANGING ATTACHMENTS

Hanging framed work in public places also carries with it certain special problems, such as burglary. This danger is best offset by the use of wallplates. Usually in brass, these fitments have three holes in them. Two attach the plate to the back of the frame by means of screws, and the other secures the subject to the wall. Two or four plates are usually sufficient to fix the picture firmly in place and deter would-be chance burglars. There are more sophisticated anti-theft devices that do much the same job, and are less obtrusive; however, the fact that the wallplate is visible is possibly as important as the fact that it is holding the picture firmly to the wall.

In a gallery, the requirements for hanging are entirely different. The walls must remain free of nails and be smart at the same time. The hanging method must be quick and relatively easy. It must also be flexible and capable of handling many and varied sizes and weights of pictures. To this end several manufacturers have produced purpose-designed hanging systems of clever design and great versatility. They involve the use of special clips, wires, and so on, that are quick, strong and durable in use. Their specific design is of no relevance to us here; suffice it to say that they are well worth considering, particularly if you are setting up a gallery from scratch.

The simplest and most basic means of hanging is two screw eyes in the back of the frame, with a double length of strong cord strung between the two fairly tightly. For heavier subjects, substitute picture wire for the cord. This is a rust-proof, malleable, braided wire of varying thickness; it is probably getting rather old-fashioned these days because of the greater availability of enormously strong thin nylon cord. There are more than enough cords, wires, and chains to choose from, and it is really a matter of common sense picking the most suitable.

Methods of attaching them to the picture are much more complex and deserve appropriate attention. The screw eye is available in 15 sizes and in zinc or brass finish, and it screws into the back of the molding. It is customarily located one-third of the way down from the top edge of the frame. (Some framers prefer the screw ring, a variant of the screw eye with a split ring attached to the eye.) After the humble screw eye comes the D-ring, which, because it is fixed to the frame with one or more screws, is considerably more secure and is, therefore, recommended for heavy art. The screw eye or screw ring can be subjected to sideways stress that may eventually tear the screw eye out of the frame if it has been used in an unsuitable situation. The D-ring's method of anchorage removes this possibility. The two-hole version of the D-ring improves the anchorage even more. Use round or cheese-head screws with D-rings rather than the countersunk variety; they look much neater and are easier to use, particularly in the smaller sizes.

The D-ring can be fixed to the backing board of the frame by means of rivets if the section profile of the molding is of insufficient strength to support the weight of its contents. (This is a situation which really should not arise with timber moldings because, if a molding of slim proportions is needed for a particular job, extruded aluminum is really the better candidate.)

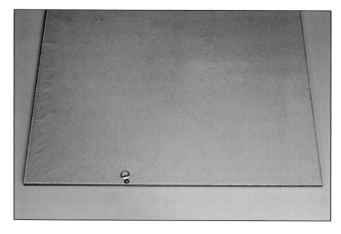

This is a surprisingly strong method of attaching the D-rings and can be used on quite large and heavy jobs. The limitations on the use of bifurcated rivets are imposed by their size; their rather short length means that they are restricted to use on relatively thin materials such as hardboard (the

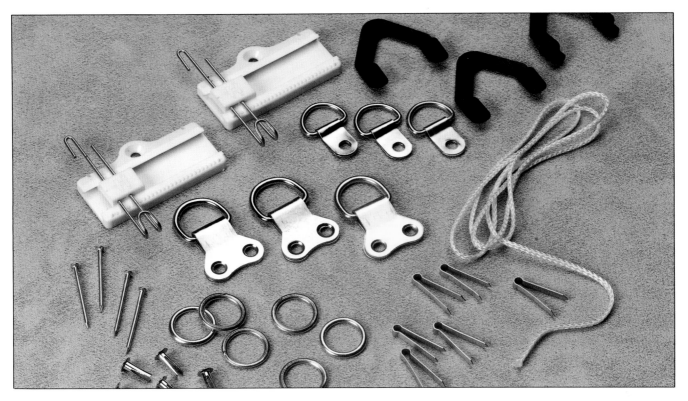

*A selection of hanging devices showing D rings; rings and clips, molded plastic fixings and an "H hanger", which allows adjustment of the position of a picture once it has been hung.*

thicker-stemmed rivets, which *are* longer, tend to be too big for the holes in the D-ring plate).

For much lighter jobs, the ring and clip is very useful. This is a metal ring with a flat anchoring piece folded around it. Generally used in light photographic-type framing situations, the ring and

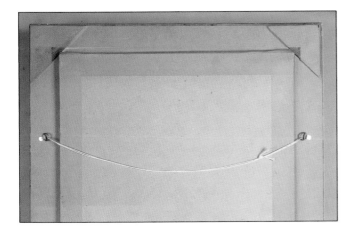

clip is passed through appropriate holes in the backing, and the clip is spread and flattened in much the same way as the bifurcated rivet. As extra security, a piece of masking tape is stuck

over the flattened clip, to prevent it from pulling back through the holes.

In many lightweight framing situations, the hanging anchorage on the picture can be made in the backing. Sometimes, for a professional framer in a mass-production situation, one carefully-positioned hanging device may suffice. There is a myriad different types of these on the market and the range grows daily. Most consist of a molded plastic shape, usually triangular, with two lugs that pass through the backing to anchor it in place. When picking a suitable type, study carefully how it is fitted. Sometimes this is a surprisingly complicated operation.

The most effective way of securing picture cord is to pass it backwards and forwards through the anchorage points. Tie it off centre, so that the knot does not get in the way of the wall hook.

Wire may be used in the same way or twisted around itself after passing through the anchorage. Be sure to test the security of either method before hanging unsupported.

# RIBBONS AND BOWS

*T*he hanging point on the wall is a subject with just as many variations. Apart from the nail, the simplest hanging item is the hook. Purpose-designed types are usually made from brass-plated steel and come complete with their own large-headed and suitably hardened pins. Designed for use mainly on plaster-covered walls and softer building materials, this type is very widely used in domestic situations for general light- to medium-weight hanging duties.

Heavier requirements in the home will involve either the wall being drilled and plugged, or suspending the subject from a picture-rail. If the suspension needs to be unobtrusive, high-breaking-strain fishing line is a good choice as it is enormously strong and yet so thin as to be almost invisible against a patterned wallpaper. The line may be either strung to a central hanging hook on the rail, or (for added security) two separate hooks may be used with the picture being suspended from either side of the frame. This method has to be much more precise when setting the lengths of the two suspension pieces, but deserves to be considered if an excessively large and heavy piece is being hung.

If the piece is obviously beyond even this capability, then wire and even chain must be evaluated. When using chain with a picture-rail, the Victorians had the idea, when it became impossible to hide it, of emphasizing the hanging chain by decorating it with various materials such as ribbon. They even went to the lengths of adding bows, and very attractive they look, where the surroundings allow.

*The use of bows, rosettes and ribbons not only disguises the hanging device but also adds interest to the decor of a room. In the bedroom the blue bows pick up the color and design of the bedlinen. Decorative cord looped into bows makes a prominent feature of a group of five pictures and the red bows draw attention to four small pictures.*

Elizabeth Whiting & Associates

Elizabeth Whiting & Associates

# STACKING PICTURES

*A*gain, when using a picture-rail, if you carefully work out the various lengths of cord or line, a series of pictures may be "stacked" one above another and hung from a single hook. Unobtrusive fishing line is essential for this type of hanging.

Alternatively, if the pictures are sufficiently light in weight, each picture can be hung from the one above it, thus reducing the amount of line on show. Both these methods need careful arranging and should be considered only when the grouping is unlikely to be moved for some considerable time. The other advantage of this system is that it removes the need for defacing the walls with nail holes – a serious problem in some older houses where the wall plaster is perhaps not too sound.

*Various methods of stacking pictures are shown in the photographs. In one, chains are used to suspend the pictures in pairs from the picture rail; in another a decorative cord allows two pictures to be hung from one hook and in the third, the pictures have their own cords but are hung from a single hook.*

# DRAMATIC GROUPS

*I*f you have a series of pictures, you can emphasize the uniformity of their subject matter and shape by hanging them together in a formal grouping. Position them with care, so that they are exactly aligned and the space between each picture is constant.

This treatment is best for bold subjects, when they will make a dramatic focal point in a room. However, they can tend to give the room the look of a public picture gallery unless they are displayed above an interesting piece of furniture, which will have the effect of integrating them with the rest of the decor of the room.

Elizabeth Whiting & Associates

Elizabeth Whiting & Associates

*These pictures have all been framed and hung for maximum impact, whether
close-framed to leave the images to speak for themselves or with black frame and
wide, white mat (mount) to add to the drama of the artwork. Note the off-center
cut-out in the three frames above to allow for a title at the side of the image.*

# *I*NFORMAL *A*RRANGEMENTS

Elizabeth Whiting & Associates

*G*roups of pictures in a mixture of sizes and shapes and with differing subjects can work well together provided there is an underlying structure to their arrangement on the wall.

When assembling the design, begin with a horizontal or vertical line and position the picture along it. You can either align one edge of the frames along this invisible line or place the pictures so that the line is running through the middle of each image.

Alternatively, you can fill the whole of a small wall space with pictures, aligning the outside edges of the frames with the shape of the wall itself.

Different types of frames can be mixed together: antique with modern, plain with decorative, narrow with broad, but a frame should not stand out against the general style of the interior design. A shiny aluminum frame could look out of place in a room completely decorated with antique furniture, unless it is specifically designed as an intentional contrast.

Elizabeth Whiting & Associates

The group of pictures on the library wall has been arranged around an imagined cross. The top and bottom edges of the frames are aligned along the horizontal bar of the cross and the vertical goes through the center of the images. The nine botanical prints are hung so that the tops of the frames align in each row. In the living room opposite the different subjects, sizes and shapes of the pictures have been formed into a coherent group by arranging them to follow the outlines of the hearth.

Elizabeth Whiting & Associates

# LARGE PAINTINGS

*L*arge pictures need space around them, both wall space and room space. Hung in a small room they will accentuate the lack of space, and look cramped. They need to be viewed at a sufficient distance, so that the whole image can be taken in, and are also best displayed at eye-level, again for ease of viewing. It is a common mistake to hang pictures too high.

Wherever they are hung they will provide a focal point, so choose carefully where you position them within the room. Hang them, for example, so that they are the first thing that is seen on entering the room or so that they can be viewed at leisure when sitting.

Test the fixings on both wall and picture before hanging a heavy painting unsupported.

Elizabeth Whiting & Associates

Elizabeth Whiting & Associates

*Elizabeth Whiting & Associates*

*These impressive paintings have all been given a position of importance within the room, whether hung above the fireplace, on a plain wall or on a specially-designed shelf. They are all positioned to make the best of the natural daylight.*

# PAIRS

*I*f you have two pictures neither of which is more than average size, they will look more effective together than hung on separate walls. A pair of pictures of the same size tends to need a third element to bring it to life. The pictures could be hung on either side of a small window or a light fitting or they could be hung above a low piece of furniture.

Two pictures of different sizes positioned together have enough interest in the shapes created to be able to hang freely on a wall away from any room features.

Elizabeth Whiting & Associates

Lars Hallen

*Two pale pencil illustrations gain from being placed next to each other in
identical frames. The positioning of the two prints on either side of the wall light
is entirely in keeping with the formal style of the dining room, and the small
picture becomes a much more interesting feature when placed
beside a larger frame.*

# ROOM SETS

## *Kitchens and Dining Rooms*

*T*he previous pages have mainly dealt with pictures hung in the reception rooms of a house. Pictures can, of course, be hung in any room, although thought should be given to the environmental conditions if the art is precious. Heat, light and damp all cause problems in the long term (as described in the chapter on conservation and restoration). Kitchens and bathrooms are not good places for valued images.

Where to hang what is also a subject that requires careful thought. It doesn't always follow that just because a particular picture is liked it will fit in anywhere. Different rooms suit different subjects. Bright and cheerful prints and posters work well in a kitchen, as well as the more obvious food-related images.

Dining rooms need subjects of interest but nothing too overwhelming, so that the pictures bear being looked at over a period of time but are not distracting.

*Pictures of food, posters, old advertisements, even a box frame containing dried*
*foods, are appropriate subjects for the kitchen. The dining room has a large*
*collection of old photographs adding interest and character to the room.*

# ROOM SETS

## *Bedrooms*

W hen deciding on pictures for a bedroom, you have a choice of whether they will be seen from the bed or whether they will be hung above the bed as part of the daytime decor of the room. This is a room where fabrics are the focal point, and where a restful atmosphere is important, so choose a soft approach either in the subject matter or in the style of hanging. As this is a room in constant use, ensure that the image of a single picture is sufficiently interesting to bear scrutiny every day or hang a group of pictures, so that there is a variety of subjects on view.

*Suitably restful approaches to hanging pictures in the bedroom can include adding ribbons and bows in fabric to match the bedlinen, hanging a large collection of flower prints, or echoing the general color scheme within the framed image.*

Fritz von der Schulenburg/Mimmi O'Connell

Elizabeth Whiting & Associates

# LIGHTING

Although lighting is extremely important to pictures, it is not always possible to arrange everything so that the subject is lit to perfection. But think twice about hanging dark subjects in corners away from light; and large glazed subjects opposite large windows will be ruined by reflections.

Individual artificial lighting works well with particular subjects, such as family portraits, particularly in oil. It is very easy, however, to illuminate too brightly – a painting can be changed totally by harsh light. It is much better to have a soft glow playing on the subject. Picture lights are an acquired taste and can look effective in certain situations – though more for their appearance than for the quality of light that they may give. The deep shadows they throw underneath the frame are undesirable and also affect the siting of subjects immediately below them. Better, perhaps, is the softer and more general effect given by specifically sited spot lights.

Careful consideration of the different types of bulbs available also pays dividends. In the gallery situation the requirements are entirely different from those in the home. In a gallery what is needed is good general illumination that is also easy on the eyes. A well-thought-out system of multiple-spotlight tracking is possibly the best answer, so long as the individual lights may be directed to the appropriate area.

Natural daylight is, of course, the best illumination of all, and every possible advantage should be taken of it in the gallery. Roof glass is excellent for showing off pictures to their best effect, and good window area comes a close second. Remember, though, that the weather is not always predictable, particularly in Britain, and so a good system of artificial light is vital even in the best naturally lit gallery.

In gallery hanging, the most important feature after the lighting is the background the subjects are displayed against. This must always be neutral in texture and calm in color. The worst color against which to hang pictures is white. Muted grays and browns are much easier on the eye, and even black is better than white. Textures such as hessian are pleasing when using a hanging system, and loop nylon is available in several restrained colors. A soft, light muddy-brown is one of the best colors for a gallery wall. If you get the shade right for the particular location, the walls seem virtually to disappear when the pictures are hung.

A remarkable example of imaginative hanging is at Lindisfarne Castle on Holy Island in Northumberland, England. In the dining hall, which is part of the old dungeon system and has an arched, vaulted ceiling, one end wall is painted a striking shade of deep purple, and in its center is hung a baroque mirror in a Celtic-patterned silver frame. In daylight the effect is startling enough; at night, by candlelight, the wall disappears and the mirror seems to hang suspended in mid-air.

Elizabeth Whiting & Associates

*Pictures can be individually lit either by an integral picture light or by a specially-positioned spotlight.*

Elizabeth Whiting & Associates

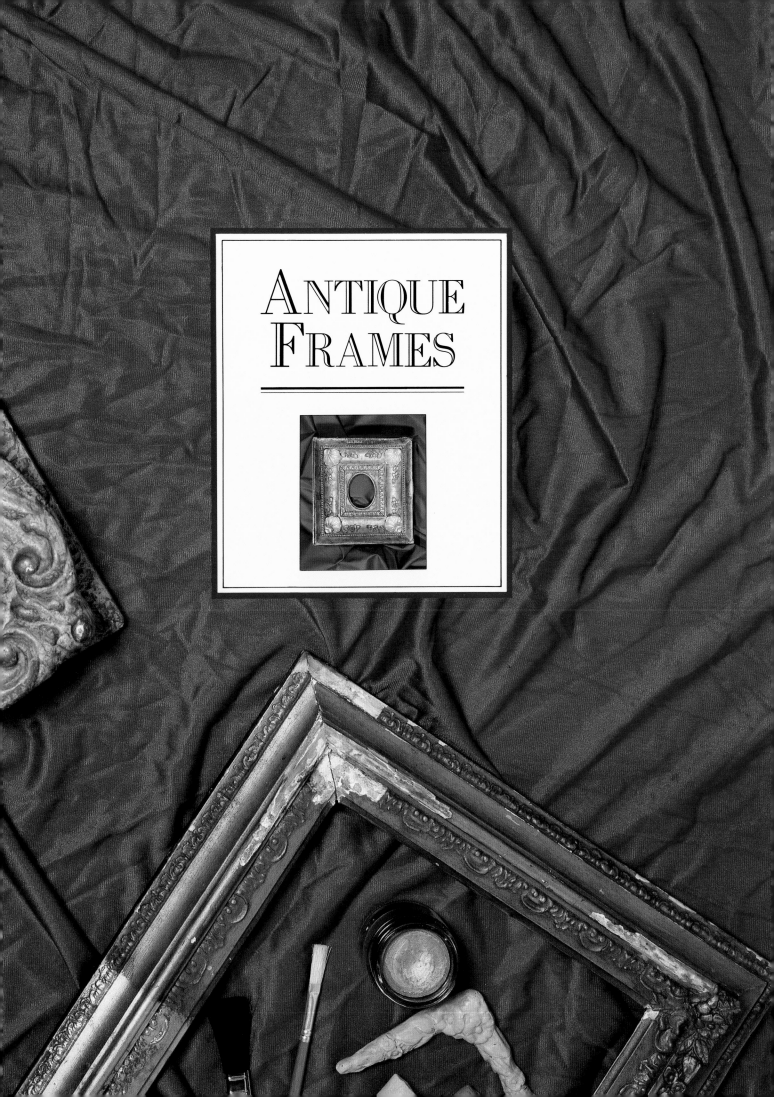

# EARLY EXAMPLES

Picture frames have been used at least since the 13th century and probably before that. The early examples, found mainly in churches and monasteries, were intended to match their often ornate surroundings and consequently were of extremely high quality created by skilled craftsmen. Their techniques were more akin to joinery than to picture framing as we know it today, and they used the sorts of joints found in furniture construction rather than the mitered-corner system that we are familiar with. As a result, quite a few have survived the ravages of war and religious upheavals. Ranging in size from the tiny examples found in icons of the 13th and 14th centuries to the gigantic mirror frames of the 18th, they are not only beautiful and superbly made but also of high commercial value. The few empty frames of great craftsmanship and undisputed age that come onto the market are usually bought to have mirrors fitted into them.

If an antique frame is completely original and undamaged, then it is best left alone: there is no substitute for the patina of age.

If you contemplate buying an antique frame of genuine quality for yourself, treat it like any other antique, balancing its condition against price. If the example that you are interested in is in apparently near-perfect condition, fine scrutiny is in order, especially if the price is high. Look for tell-tale marks, such as evidence of a saw being used to remove certain parts to match gaps in other parts occasioned by wear and tear. The use of stains, paints, and dirt may also indicate attempts to disguise damage. Good restorers of old frames are few and far between, but they are growing in number.

*These early examples of antique frames originally hung in churches but are now all museum pieces. The earliest (top left) is from the 13th century. The triptych (left) survives from the 14th century and the Russian icon is 16th century. In the 18th century classic frames came under the rococo influence and became extremely ornate. The mirror (right) was made around 1740.*

# REPAIRING AN ORNATE MOLDING

*C*uriously, the easiest type of frame to repair is the highly ornate variety, as there is nearly always some of the pattern remaining that can be copied or from which a mold can be made. For casting intricate patterns you can use Plasticine for a mold, as follows:

*1* Soften the Plasticine first in hot water to make it pliable.

*2* While the Plasticine is warming, liberally dust the area that the mold is to be taken from with powdered chalk, so that the Plasticine will lift easily after taking the imprint.

*3* Press the soft Plasticine carefully into the molding, applying firm pressure from all angles to ensure the pattern is faithfully reproduced.

*4* Leave it to cool slightly, and then carefully remove the mold. Some bending of the Plasticine is inevitable but will do no harm as long as it is returned to its original shape as soon as possible after removal.

*5* Now put the mold in the refrigerator for an hour or two so that the Plasticine sets rock-hard.

*6* For the casting material, two-part epoxy putty is ideal. It casts well, sets hard in a few hours, and can be sanded, sawn, and shaped when cured. It is also ideal for freehand forming of detail that cannot be cast-molded for one reason or another. A bit more expensive than the more traditional gesso-whitening-putty mixtures, epoxy putty is a lot more convenient, much less messy, and much stronger in its final form.

7 To fix the newly-molded section to the frame, use a wood glue. Always leave any pieces of the original molding in place and file or sand the new piece to fit. Add the wood glue to the frame and the new piece. Leave for a few minutes, then press together.

Finishing the final repair is just as important as the reconstruction of damaged or missing areas. It requires careful study of the effects of age on different materials, particularly gold leaf. Probably the most obvious repair is that on a leafed object. When the new leaf is applied to the repair, it shines out like a beacon and so will need to be "aged" and toned down. Patching is a very difficult task and should be used only if the result is predictable. Be prepared to refinish the entire frame to ensure an even finish, remembering to apply suitable aging (*see page 91*).

"Restoring" is probably a misleading term to use in connection with old frames, but "repairing" also lacks the correct descriptive quality for what is being achieved. Suffice it to say that generally what is required is that the frame, when repaired and complete, will have the appearance of being in extremely good *original* condition – not new. It is all too easy to fall into the trap of making perfect something of which the patina of age is an intrinsic part.

Plain frames with little or no ornate decoration are far more difficult to repair. Usually, you need to strip off all applied material in order to get down to a stable base from which to work, which is a time-consuming job. By far the most commonly repaired frames are the swept type (*see page 74*).

Veneered frames suffer the most from the ravages of time, as they are the most vulnerable to damp and variations of temperature. If the veneer has lifted but is intact, modern glues and veneering irons will soon remedy the problem. But missing veneer usually signifies real trouble. Veneer has changed considerably over the years, so obtaining the exact match for an old veneer is almost impossible. One of the problems is the thickness of the veneer. Over the years the machinery for cutting veneers has become more and more sophisticated, and consequently veneers are nowadays much thinner than formerly. Another problem is matching the varieties of timber. A couple of hundred years ago timber was plentiful and available in great variety. The years since then have seen the demise of whole forests of certain types of timber. In the 18th century, for instance, bird's-eye maple veneer was a favorite among high-class framers, and its almost translucent honey-gold color graced countless engravings and watercolors. If you try to match that veneer with a modern equivalent, the latter seems to lack that "lit from within" quality of the older frame.

# ANTIQUE VARIATIONS

*An original Oxford frame round a modern embroidery.*

A design that seems to be rarer than most today is the "Oxford" frame. This frame has no miters at the corners, but instead has simple halved joints, familiar to the carpenter, but with the ends of both the vertical and horizontal moldings continuing out from the corners of the frame for two or three inches.

Usually quite small, Oxford frames are generally found on rustic subjects like samplers and sentimental embroideries such as "Home Sweet Home." Sometimes they are modern fakes, but the latter are usually quite easy to identify because most have the rabbet (rebate) running the full length of the molding, whereas the genuine article will have a rabbet (rebate) only on the molding within the four sides, not on the projecting pieces.

The design of these charming examples of antique frames arose out of purely practical considerations, with very little regard for esthetics. The village carpenter or furniture-maker would have been approached to make a frame, and, being a wood craftsman, joined the four pieces of oak, or whatever, in the simplest way

he knew how – by using a halved joint, which has timber on both sides of the joint – whence the "Oxford" frame. The name simply denotes that this type was most common in that town; examples are to be found all over Britain.

Antique frames have not always been produced exclusively by pictures framers: silversmiths and jewelers have produced their share over the years, and some very fine examples there are, too. Usually they were used for miniatures and cameos, and most commonly consisted of beaten and shaped sheet silver on a wooden core; but some very valuable examples can also be found in solid cast silver.

The design of picture-frame moldings has not changed significantly over the centuries, but the development of highly sophisticated spraying and finishing equipment over the past 20 years has resulted in the introduction of many new and interesting surface effects. No doubt the future will see many more advances and innovations in picture framing as new technologies come to the aid of the framer.

Robert Harding

*A selection of silver frames made between 1898 and 1909.*

# CONSERVATION AND RESTORATION

# PAINTINGS

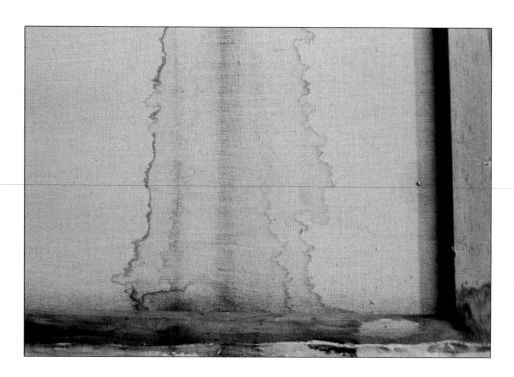

*C*onservation is the practice of caring for art. It includes all the techniques and procedures used to retard the natural deterioration that comes with age. Restoration is the practice of repairing damage. All art needs conservation, most will sooner or later also require some restoration.

All conservation and restoration work should be reversible. Nothing should be done that cannot be undone. The goal of conservation is to extend the life of the art; that of restoration to hide the visual distractions of damage. Neither conservation nor restoration should change the artist's original concept.

Because of the differences in the materials, methods of application and type of supports used, the conservation and restoration of paintings and art on paper have been separated.

Conservation and restoration are best done professionally. But it is important to be able to recognize condition and potential problems. The condition of a painting is best checked out of the frame. It is important to examine the edges, as well as the face and back. Being able to recognize the age, period, or style as well as the material composition of a painting is helpful. The more information you have the better.

Examine the face of the painting, look at it directly and at an angle. Look for consistency. The surface may be dull or with a high gloss. It may have a yellow, brown, or gray overtone. There may be a visible surface contamination of dust, smoke, or dirt. The surfaces of unvarnished paintings are most often dull or flat. A varnished surface can be anything from almost dull to a high gloss. Regardless of the condition of the surface, there should be a consistency. An inconsistent surface is the clue that something has changed. A change in the surface can be an indication of a potential problem or it may indicate previous restoration.

All oil paintings have surface cracks. Cracks are part of the aging process. Numerous or large cracks appearing in a localized area can indicate a problem. Cracks that are cupping or beginning to curl at the edges also indicate a problem. When paint cracks and begins to cup or curl, it has lost its bond to the underpaint and will eventually flake.

There may be areas that look like cracking, but that in fact are caused by the artist's materials or techniques. This condition of paint shrinkage may be distracting to look at but is most often not damaging.

Look at the back. The stretchers to which the canvas is attached should not be twisted, cracked, or split. They should not be bowed. Large canvasses should have a center bar for additional support. The stretchers should be angled on the canvas side so that the canvas when pulled tight will not touch. All four corners should be expandable in both directions independently and have keys in place. The stretchers should not be expanded excessively, but the canvas should be taut.

Look for water stains, as shown in the photograph on the previous page; paintings that have been exposed to excessive moisture often begin to flake at a later time. Look for patches: they can indicate areas of damage and restoration work. Look for accumulation of dust and dirt between the stretchers and the canvas. Hold the canvas up to a light; viewing from the back will reveal pin holes, flaking, and weak spots not seen from the front. Check the tack edges of the canvas. Old canvas becomes dry and brittle and will tear easily.

A professional examination usually includes the use of ultraviolet light, commonly called a black light. In a darkroom, a black light fluoresces all oils, paint pigments, and other surface materials which reflect differently. Even areas of the same material applied at different times will most often show up. A restored area will likely be seen as darker tones of blue violet. However, if restoration has been done to hide something, techniques can be employed to fool the black light. Also, the artist's original techniques may have been inconsistent. Black light readings can be difficult to evaluate by themselves. But a black light

examination almost always provides a clue as to where to look for real or suspected problems.

## Paint

Artist's oil paint is made to be applied to a primed surface. It may be thinned and layered or mixed with compatible mediums, such as a drier to speed up the drying time. These additions to the paint's original formula alter its working properties. The changes are important to the artist as they help create the desired effects.

Changes in paint consistency can cause problems. When a new layer of paint is applied over a layer of paint that has not yet dried, the overpaint may dry more quickly. When the underpaint dries it shrinks, causing the overpaint to crack, separate, and show the underpaint.

Time, temperature, and humidity all affect a painting as it ages. As paint dries it becomes harder, less plastic, and over time even brittle. As this happens, small cracks develop. This is considered normal aging. If the canvas is not properly stretched or the environmental conditions are extreme, the changes can be damaging. Drying paint can shrink the canvas. Additional cracking and flaking can occur, as shown in the photograph.

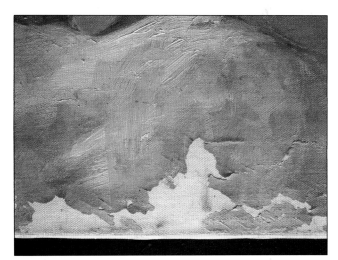

## The Varnish

Differences in paint consistency can alter our perception of its color. We see color as light reflected from a surface; if the surface varies, so will the reflection. It is important that the surface be consistent. Dull, dark colors all appear to be black. A coat of picture varnish gives life to dark colors. A properly varnished painting need not have a high gloss reflective surface. The type of varnish and method of application will control the reflective qualities. Varnish also protects the painted surface. Any accumulation of smoke or dirt rests on the varnish, not on the paint. The surface can be cleaned without direct contact with the paint. Picture varnish used for paintings is formulated for its protective qualities as well as for easy removal. Using other types of varnish may cause permanent damage.

A painting should not be revarnished without first being cleaned. Revarnishing over surface dirt only creates a darker surface that can obscure the artist's work.

A painting should not be framed before the paint or varnish is dry. Paintings should not be pressed tightly into the rebate of the frame. Paintings should never be varnished while still in the frame.

All of these things can cause the painting and the frame to adhere to each other, which can cause damage to the painting when it is removed.

## Stretchers

Stretchers are the foundation of a traditional painting on canvas. They should be made of good wood with a clean, straight grain that will not crack, twist, or bow. The dimensions should be in proportion to the span. They should not bend when tension is applied stretching a canvas. Each corner should be expandable in both directions independently (*see diagram*). The size of painting and the dimensions of the stretchers will dictate when a center bar is necessary. Large paintings should have cross bars for additional support. All additional bars should be expandable (*see diagram*). The stretchers must provide a strong foundation for the canvas. A proper set will be expandable and hold the canvas under tension without twisting or bending.

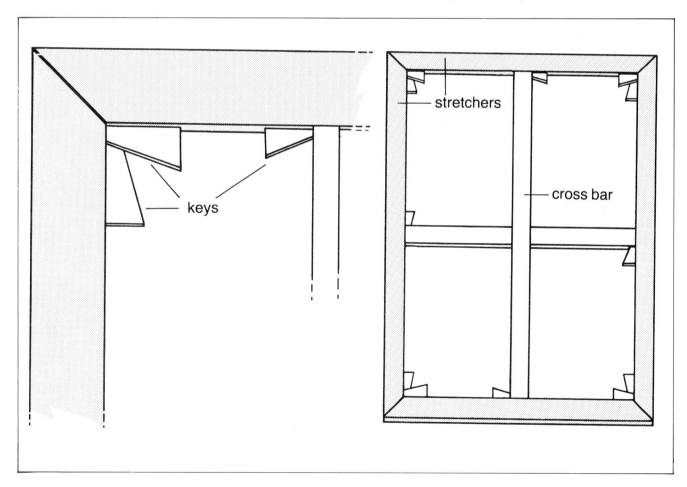

keys

stretchers

cross bar

## The canvas

The canvas is the support for the art. It is a woven material, most often cotton or linen, although jute is also used. The weave of the fabric consists of threads interlaced at right angles, one thread (the weft) interlaced back and forth across a set of lengthwise threads (the warp). Most weaves do not stretch equally in both directions. The warp, being of greater length, will stretch more than the weft. This is the reason all stretcher parts must expand independently, so that they can apply equal tension to both sets of threads – a fact that is overlooked by some stretcher designs even today.

The initial stretching of a canvas should produce a tight, evenly-tensioned surface without using the keys. There should be no waviness in the corners or along the sides, as this indicates that the stretching tension was uneven. The photograph below shows the surface problems that can occur when the stretchers are incorrectly used. The severe cracking in the center is caused by humidity. The life of a canvas depends on its type of fiber and care. A stretched canvas is constantly changing in response to environmental temperature and humidity. As canvas ages, it becomes dry and brittle, loses its initial strength, and becomes very susceptible to damage by contact.

Canvas may also be adhered to a solid support, such as cardboard or hardboard. Canvas prepared in this manner is susceptible to all the problems of a stretched surface as well as those that can affect the material the canvas has been mounted on. In these cases, humidity can cause not only many of the problems of a stretched canvas, but also may affect the adhesive by which the canvas has been fixed to its support.

## Ground

Both canvas and wood panels may have preliminary coatings as a base for the painting. Size and ground coats seal the supports and prevent them from absorbing the paint. Traditional size and ground formulas are water soluble, making them very susceptible to damage from moisture. Excessive moisture can destroy them and cause paint loss. Excessive moisture can also shrink the canvas. Wood panels or boards can warp and crack.

# PAINTINGS

## *Conservation and Restoration*

As a canvas ages it becomes brittle, loses its strength, and is susceptible to damage from contact and environmental changes. The canvas or its support deteriorates long before the paint. A stretched canvas is under tension and the pull should be even in all directions, so that its reaction to environmental changes will be consistent. Even a small tear in a canvas requires a full lining to maintain its integrity. The life of a painting can be extended by a new support. A lining is the process whereby the painting and its support are attached to another canvas or support.

Temporary patches and quick fixes should be avoided. First, you will probably succumb to the temptation to regard the repair as permanent – which it certainly is not. Indeed, if left for long, such patches can become a source of other forms of damage. Second, patches can interfere with the normal movement of the canvas. In time the patch, when viewed from the front, shows as an embossed area that can have detrimental effects on the painted surface. Sometimes the damage created by a temporary patch will be irreversible even by the most skilled conservator, as shown in the series of three photographs below. The original damage to

the painting was patched. After lining and cleaning, the true damage can be seen.

The same problems may be caused by other things being glued to the back of the canvas, such as information about the painting or the artist. When any area is restricted, it will react to the environment differently. This affects the canvas and the painted surface.

Any problem should be treated as soon as possible. Tears left untreated allow the canvas to shrink. It can never be restretched and the repair becomes more difficult.

The most common reasons for paint to flake are that the ground has deteriorated and lost its bond, or the paint is not adhering to the ground or underpaint. If the problem is with the ground it can be treated from the back. A wax lining will most often provide consolidation of the paint, ground, and canvas.

If, however, the flaking is between paint layers or between paint and ground, the problem may be more difficult or impossible to treat, as there is no way to work in between the layers of paint.

There are two basic methods of attaching an old canvas to a new support – glue lining and wax

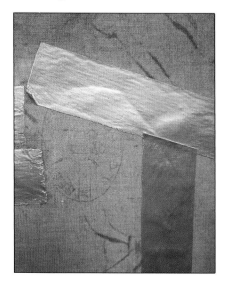

lining. Originally, the glue method employed hot rabbitskin glue as the bonding medium. This has been largely superseded by the wax method which employs a wax-resin adhesive. Regardless of the method, the basic preparation work is the same.

The old canvas is removed from the stretchers and the back is cleaned. There are two opinions on this procedure. One holds that the tacks should be removed and that the tack edges should be left on the canvas. The other recommends that the canvas be cut at the fold and the tack edges discarded. Leaving the tack edges on the canvas presents several problems. First, the fold can never be completely flattened, and this affects areas on both sides of it. Second, when the lined canvas is restretched the two canvases will not bend equally. The reason for expandable stretchers is to keep the canvas taut. Any unevenness in the bonding of the two canvases or in their ability to stretch equally can cause problems.

After lining and before restretching, the painting is cleaned. In the past, all manner of things have been used to clean or brighten a painting's surface. For example, there are records of wetting the surface with horse urine and then rinsing it off with clean water. Placing the painting in direct sunlight for a few days was a remedy for darkened varnish. Helpful hints and household remedies called for the use of a fresh-cut potato, an onion, a handful of bread, or a side of bacon. All of these briefly produced a shiny surface – but then dried, leaving a film of residue and whatever dust it had collected.

If this treatment were repeated, the effect was that the residue eventually obscured the color and details of the painting.

Oils, especially linseed oil, were sometimes used to coat the surface of paintings in the belief that they would keep the paint soft and retard surface cracking. In fact, they merely created a tacky surface that collected more dust and dirt.

Cleaning paintings is really a job for the expert, but it can produce exciting results – as the series of photographs on the right demonstrates. All conservation and restoration procedures involve

risks. Just because a particular method worked on one painting is no guarantee that it will work on another. Every painting is more or less unique in terms of its combination of pigments, colors, techniques of application, age, condition of the canvas and ground, and all the potentially harmful environmental influences it has been subjected to since the artist put paint to canvas. All these things must be considered in any conservation or restoration treatment.

# ART ON PAPER

The term "art on paper" describes all art that uses paper as a support. This includes all paintings and drawings as well as all types of printed art, both original and in reproduction.

Paper was first made in China in the second century. In the twelfth century, paper was made from cotton and linen rags in Europe. When the supplies of available rags could no longer meet the growing demand for paper, other materials were tried as substitutes.

In the nineteenth century, wood pulp was found to be suitable, available in large quantities, and relatively cheap, and became the basis of a major industry. It was not until the 1950s that the full effects of the change in paper composition were recognized.

The composition of wood, as well as the chemicals used in manufacturing, produce papers and cardboards that deteriorate more quickly than rag-based papers. Methods of purification have been developed to increase the life of wood pulp papers and boards. These papers are generally called "acid-free," "archival," or "pH neutral," and usually have a higher than neutral alkaline content that helps resist or slow the affects of deterioration. The protection provided by acid-free materials can vary depending upon use and conditions, and even the best materials will not last forever.

## ART ON PAPER

The environment has a greater visual effect on paper than on paintings. Paper visibly reacts to both temperature and humidity, which cause it to expand and contract. It is unrealistic to expect paper always to be flat, even when it is framed.

To check the condition of art on paper properly, it must be unframed. The overall condition is important. Look at the general condition of the paper, checking for acid burns or any discolorations. Examine the surface for scratches, areas of ink flaking, and folds, bends, or creases in the paper. Look along the margins for dirty areas, finger prints, tears, and abrasions. Check the back for any tape or framing and mending materials. If the art has embossed areas, hold it up to the light; looking from the back, check the embossing for weak, thin, or cut edges.

### Framing

Beware of claims such as "framed to museum standards" or "conservation framed." These are general statements open to interpretation. As far as I know, there is no general museum standard; each sets its own. "Conservation" means to save or protect, but not everyone agrees as to exactly what that means.

Mounting and framing should not restrict the expansion and contraction of paper. If this natural response to the environment is restricted, the paper will buckle and became wavy, a condition referred to as "cockling." Damage as well as cockling can also be caused by how the art is attached to the mount.

Gluing the paper only on the four corners is an example of a bad method. When the paper expands, this restricted movement causes the paper to become wavy. When the paper contracts, the pull at the corners can cause it to tear.

Any attachment that restricts the paper's normal movement creates stress that, over time, causes damage. Two methods which overcome this problem are detailed on the next page.

## H I N G I N G   A R T   O N   P A P E R

Hinging is the time-tested method of holding art in place. It requires a minimum attachment and allows unrestricted movement.

Hinging involves the use of Japanese papers and wheat-starch paste. The long fibers of Japanese papers are strong, and when the paper is torn it produces a soft edge that is ideal for hinging. The process is as follows:

1.  Mix the dry wheat starch and water, heat, and allow to cool.

2.  Strip a sheet of Japanese paper by wetting a line along the grain. The grain or direction of the fiber of Japanese papers can be seen when looking at the paper in front of a strong light. These long strips are separated from the sheet by gently pulling the fibers apart. The strips are then separated into smaller pieces to be used as hinges.

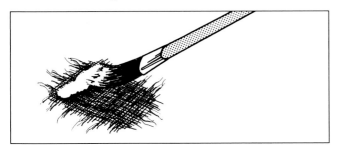

3.  Apply a small amount of cool wheat-starch paste to one feathered edge of a hinge (*see diagram*).

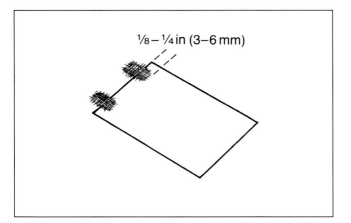

⅛–¼ in (3–6 mm)

4.  Apply the hinges to the art (*see diagram*).

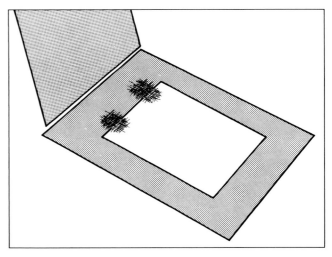

5.  Align the art on a backboard and attach the hinges to it (*see diagram*). Dry under a weight to prevent cockling.

By attaching the hinges to the art and then to the backboard, the art can be removed from the backboard without damage by simply cutting the hinges. Properly-applied hinges can also be removed from the art by re-applying moisture to the pasted area of the hinge. Both the application and removal of hinges takes some practice.

Another method of securing art on paper is to use acid-free corners. Corners require no physical attachment to the paper, and allow the paper to expand and contract. Corners can be made from Japanese or other suitable papers or they can be purchased.

The art is carefully positioned on a backboard. Each corner of the art is slightly lifted, a corner is placed on it, then returned to its position on the backboard and secured (*see diagram*).

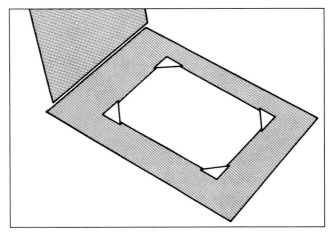

## WHAT DAMAGES
### ART ON PAPER

Art on paper is most often damaged by careless handling, environmental conditions, and framing. Light accelerates deterioration and can affect all materials: pigments fade, papers change color. Wood-pulp papers and boards used as the support or as framing materials can cause problems. The yellow-brown darkening of the material, referred to as "acid burn", is caused by elements in acidic wood-pulp paper and ultraviolet light. This combination forms deteriorating, corrosive chemicals. It can also affect acid-free papers that are in direct contact; a newspaper quickly discolors when exposed to sunlight. The two photographs below show a print before and after a period of exposure to light.

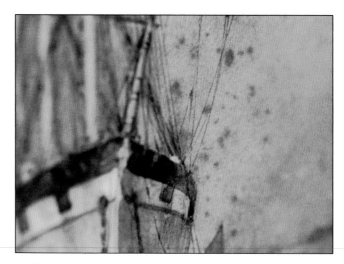

Brown spots may appear at random in selected areas or all over the art. These can be due to inherent problems in the paper, contamination from the environment or framing materials in direct contact, glue stains, or even mold growth. The effects of all of these are commonly referred to as foxing (*see photograph above*).

Mold left untreated will discolor areas and eat through the paper (*see photograph below*). Mold

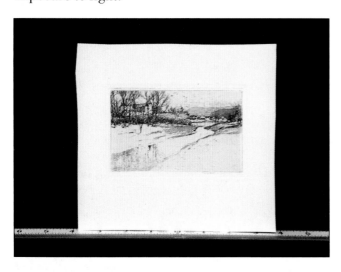

growth is accelerated by warm, dark, moist conditions.

High humidity may cause the paper to cockle or become wavy, and may even create water stains.

Using materials such as gummed tapes, masking tapes, and other self-adhesive or water-activated tapes may stain the paper as well as tear its fibers when they are removed.

Problems with art on paper should be treated as soon as possible. If left untreated, they may cause irreparable damage or even total loss.

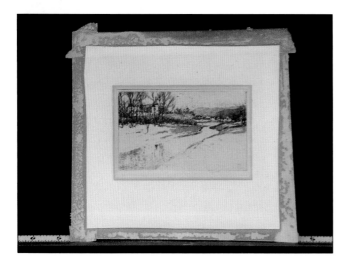

# ART ON PAPER

## Conservation and Restoration

The conservation of art on paper starts with its day-to-day care. Other problems arise mostly from its deterioration or things that happen to it. The paints and inks used on paper are more susceptible to fading than the paints used on canvas, and if they fade there is little that can be done to restore them.

Discoloration of the paper and the framing materials is likely to be the greatest problem and an indication of deterioration. This often presents itself as a yellowing or darkening of the paper (acid burn). An acidic condition can make the paper brittle, and therefore susceptible to cracks and tears.

Treatments for art on paper are a matter for an expert. They often start with a water bath. This can be followed by bleaching, appropriate rinsing, and deacidification. Then any restoration, mending, or backing can be done. The series of three photographs below and on the following page shows, first, a print acid burned by the combination of light and wood pulp paper. The second photograph shows the tide lines caused by high humidity; the third shows the art restored to its original condition.

If the paper has deteriorated or been damaged to the point that it needs additional support, it is backed, most often with another sheet of paper. There is a wide range of adhesives, backing papers and boards, and methods used by professional conservators.

Little, if anything, that can be done to art on paper can be considered totally safe. All conservation methods, materials, and procedures

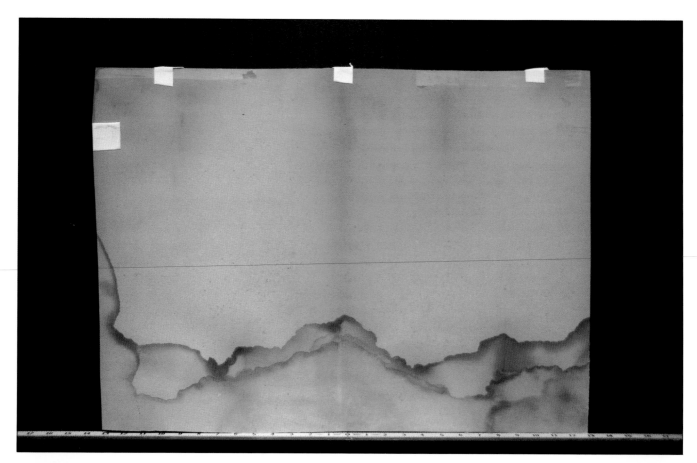

WINTER IN THE COUNTRY.—THE FARMERS HOME.

must conform to the philosophy that nothing is to be done that cannot be undone without damage to the original. Paper is fragile and highly susceptible to damage. It must be protected from the harmful effects of water, humidity, and light, and it must be carefully handled.

---

## CONCLUSION

In the field of art, qualified help can be hard to find. Information can be confusing and sometimes misleading. But sooner or later, professional help will be needed, for normal conservation, or an unexpected problem. Finding the right help is important and should be done before it is needed.

To find help, start by checking with the appropriate professional association. Such an affiliation does not always guarantee knowledge or expertise, but it does indicate a professional attitude. Check on your selection as you would a new doctor. There are many similarities in both these professions; much of the information is constantly changing, there is very little that is known absolutely. Not everyone who says they can restore art is qualified. Beware of the quick fix or cheap job; it usually involves shortcuts that create greater problems later.

Picture framers are not all the same. Framing is both a craft and an art. Most picture framers show examples of their work which may help to illustrate the results you can expect. It is important to ask questions so you thoroughly understand what is to be done. Ask about risks to the art from the materials or techniques to be used. All professionals understand your concerns, they

should be willing to discuss their background and training as well as answer specific questions about any job.

Unfortunately, all it takes to become a gallery owner, picture framer, or even a conservator is the capital to open a store. Always beware of the "know-it-all." No one lives that long.

To understand that art needs periodic care is the first step in extending its life and conserving its condition. It is important to consider not only how it looks on the wall but how it will be affected by its surroundings.

1.  The less light the better: never hang paintings in direct sunlight.

2.  High humidity areas such as bathrooms and kitchens can be detrimental.

3.  Avoid hot places or where there may be rapid temperature changes, e.g. over heat sources.

4.  Check the method of hanging as well as the attachment to the wall at least once a year.

5.  Always check the materials to be used in framing to make sure they will not cause damage.

For additional information or individual help with your art, ask a framer or conservator on whom you know you can rely. Individual items have special needs and it is important to be aware of them.

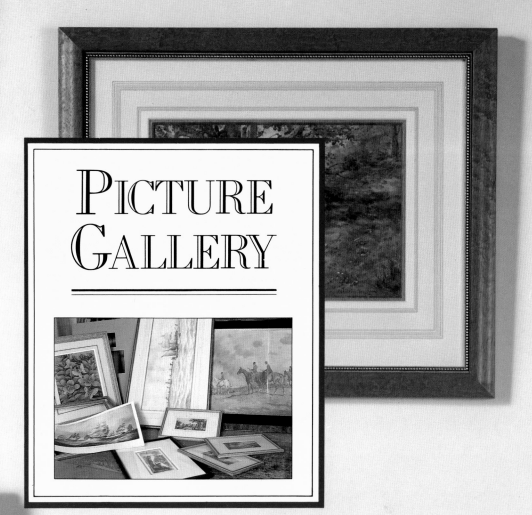

# PICTURE GALLERY

# PORTRAITS

West Midlands Arts/Alison Ross

*Nice period treatment of a subject in the pre-Raphaelite style. Well-chosen art nouveau molding.*

Author's collection

Author's collection

*Plain inner frame, hand-decorated border, with substantial outer frame for an imposing effect.*

*Single oval gold mat (mount) in gold-leafed molding of suitably grand proportions.*

*Antique carved oak frame with gold double oval mat (mount) gives an original*
*look to an old photograph.*

# BOTANICAL PAINTINGS

*Channel frame, hand-finished in crackle-glaze over green with gilding, wash-line and double mat (mount).*

*Hand varnished frame with double mat (mount), wash-line decoration on top board.*

Porter Design

*O.G. frame in polished wood with carved and gilded ribbon and stick slip with central bow. Wash-line decoration with sponged undermat (mount).*

Porter Design

*Polished ash frame, double mat (mount) with ink lines and marble paper strip.*

# REPRODUCTIONS

*Light and airy treatment, with off-white over colored board, double mat (mount). Simple but elegant molding.*

Published and manufactured by Athena International Ltd

*Simple mottled molding in keeping with the color and style of the impressionists.*

CLAUDE MONET 1840-1926 · BENEATH THE LILACS

Published and manufactured by Athena International Ltd

Published and manufactured by Athena International Ltd

*Broad wood molding leads nicely into subject. Tasteful double mat (mount) contains subject.*

*Velvet-covered mat (mount) with gold slip. Oak cushion molding with brass corners to give that opulent "hunting lodge" feel.*

# CRAFTS

R Wilkinson

*Glorious opulent feel to leafed molding and slip, to suit goldwork embroidery.*

Arcaid

*Molding with deep rabbet (rebate) formed into box frame for a three-dimensional model.*

*Double mat (mount) to keep raised embroidery clear of glass. Broad band of the undermat (mount) frames the needlework, upper board picks up on main color of stitches.*

*Simple treatment to machine embroidered picture. Circular mat (mount) in peach shade, simple and effective molding.*

# LANDSCAPES

*Pierced and carved frame on the grand scale in keeping with the subject.*

*Elegant green and gold molding perfectly frames the subject, enriching yet not distracting from the colors of the painting.*

*Frame made from a length of molding approximately 50 years old.*

*Original watercolor. Eight-line wash-line mat (mount) on 100% rag, thick
antiqued gold under mat (mount), bird's eye maple molding with
"bobble-edge" slip.*

# MODERN SUBJECTS

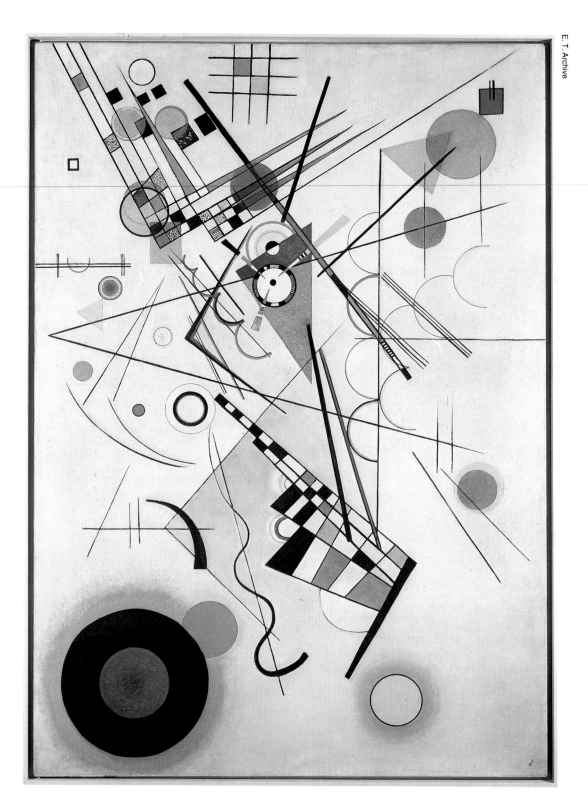

E. T. Archive

*Molding chosen to match background of painting and standing away from it,
leaving subject free from direct contact.*

Arcaid

Close-framed poster with narrow molding enhancing the
verticality of the subject.

West Midlands Arts/Alan Dyer

Plain dark wood molding to contain the riot of images
within the picture.

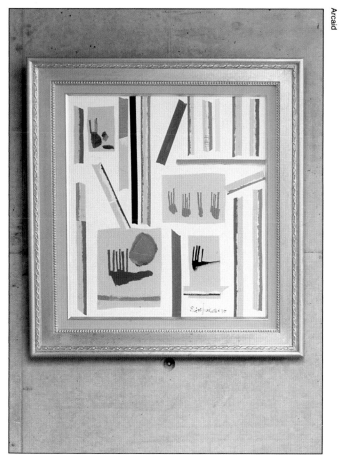

Arcaid

Mat (mount) with gold painted bevel, clean-looking gilt
molding to match the geometry of the subject.

# THE PICTURE FRAMING BUSINESS

*T*here must be few trades in which you can launch a business with such a low capital outlay and such a high expectation of making a profit.

## GENERAL OR SPECIALIZED?

What kind of business do you have in mind – general or specialized framing? If general, do you envisage mass-production work from a High Street outlet employing several experienced staff, or do you intend to stick to a one-person operation? If you have large-scale ambitions, do you want to run a completely independent business, or would you consider taking a franchise outlet as one of a chain of shops?

New businesses may need to offer a full range of services before they become established. Once past this stage, there is a vast range of options for the specialized framer. Specialization is usually more rewarding not only because of the specialty itself but also because it implies the highest standard of work and the greatest creative input. Most craft framers would much prefer making one expensive frame than ten frames, each at a tenth of the cost.

There are, of course, many different kinds of specialty. You might wish to specialize in certain types of subjects – tapestries and other needlework, for example – or in certain types of frames. Or you may wish to cater to particular types of customers; some framers, for instance, base much of their business on producing frames for artists or for publishers of limited-edition prints.

## TRAINING

There are numerous courses offering training in different aspects of picture framing, which offer an excellent opportunity to gain good practical experience in a concentrated space of time. One or two pointers as to what to look for from a course may be helpful.

Be wary of schools that are oriented around specific makes of equipment: the chances are more time will be spent on selling than on actual training. Find out whether the tutor is a practiced framer: there is no substitute for experience. Do not commit yourself to pre-paying for a course. Take a one or two-day course initially, so that you can establish whether the tutor and the course are suitable. Do not take too literally what you learn at a framing school: learn to be flexible and adapt what you learn to your own particular needs. In the specialist area of conservation, however, guidelines are important, and should be followed closely.

## STOCK CONTROL

The framer starting out in business needs to pay particular attention to stock control. Most framers carry far too large stocks of moldings, mats (mounts), glass and other basic raw materials of their trade, mainly in response to carefully orchestrated campaigns of "encouragement" by their suppliers. With the development of the regional wholesalers, however, the framer can order as much or as little as he really needs – and with the certainty that it will be delivered within a couple of days.

An even more significant check to overstocking is the "chop service", whereby moldings are delivered ready mitered to the framer and merely need assembling. This service, widely available in the United States and now gaining ground steadily in Britain, is particularly valuable to the general framer engaged on contract work. And since most of the moldings ordered from the service will be of the larger, more expensive varieties, the saving on space in the framer's molding racks will be considerable.

## PRESENTATION

Too little thought is given by the average framer to the way his or her business is presented to the customer. The showroom should not only be well designed and furnished, but should display varied examples of the framer's work as well as the usual rows of molding samples. Use natural light where possible; if the showroom is artificially lit, make sure to use color-corrected lighting: you do not want the customer to choose a frame of a particular color – only to discover that it looks completely different when the picture is hung in his or her sunny drawing room.

It goes without saying that the framer must have a complete grasp of every technique involved in making a picture frame. It will, clearly, be an additional advantage if he or she has a fairly sophisticated esthetic sense. He or she needs to be able to respond positively to the particular piece of artwork the customer has brought along and to explain to the customer why that watercolor, etching, tapestry or whatever would be seen to best advantage in a particular type, shape, color and weight of frame. To that end, it is a good idea to have in the showroom various pictures – say, a black-and-white portrait photograph, a watercolor landscape, and a piece of silk embroidery – each of which is framed in, perhaps, half a dozen different styles of molding and mat (mount). It is much easier to explain the pros and cons of a particular style of frame for a particular kind of picture if you have examples of such styles in front of you. It is also a good idea to assemble an album of color photographs showing the full range of frames you have produced for every kind of artwork. It is quite likely that the customer will find in it exactly the sort of frame and mount he or she has in mind but has been unable to describe in words.

It is important, above all, that after placing an order the customer leaves the showroom with the conviction that, although he or she has benefited from the framer's expertise, it is the customer who has chosen the style of frame he or she wants at the sort of price he or she is prepared to pay. It is then the framer's responsibility to deliver the order as specified and on time.

# GLOSSARY

**Acid-free Paper** Paper treated to resist effects of deterioration; also known as "archival" or "pH neutral" paper.

**Acrylic Paint** Paint in which the pigment is suspended in a synthetic resin.

**Agate Tool** Hand tool tipped with a semiprecious stone, used by framers to burnish molding.

**Antiquing** Conferring an aged or worn appearance on, e.g., the surface of a molding.

**Bevel** Angled or rounded edge of the aperture in a mat (mount).

**Black Light** An ultraviolet light used by picture restorers to examine artwork. In a darkroom the black light fluoresces pigments, altering their reflective properties.

**Block Mount** Piece of wood, chipboard or similar material onto which a picture is mounted.

**Bole** Fine clay of natural color used on moldings as a base for applying gold leaf; also known as gilder's clay.

**Burnish** To rub a surface with a smooth, hard material to produce a lustrous finish.

**Burnishing Bronze** Powder, laid on with size, which can be burnished to produce a finish similar to gold leaf.

**Cassetta Frame** Picture frame with a wide, flat center panel.

**Clay, Gilder's:** *see* **Bole**

**Clip-frame** arrangement by which glass, mat (mount), picture and backing board are held together by spring clips along the top, bottom, and sides of the frame.

**Close-framing** Framing without a mat (mount).

**Cockling** The buckling of art-on-paper, caused by frame or mounting method restricting paper's natural expansion and contraction.

**Cold Mounting:** *see* **Wet Mounting**

**Conservation Mounting** Use of acid-free mat (mount), glue, tape, backing board and other materials to avoid damaging valuable pictures, etc.

**Cullet** Scrap glass.

**Cutch, Gilder's** Leather-covered pad for handling sheets of gold leaf in water gilding.

**Damask** Silk, linen or other fabric with figured pattern woven into it.

**Découpage** (French = "cutting out") Pictures that have three-dimensional depth but require a mat (mount) when framed.

**Diffused-reflection Glass** Non-reflective glass. Its property of diffusing an image viewed through the glass can limit the use of multiple mats (mounts) where DRG is fitted.

**Distressing** Deliberate superficial damaging of an object such as a picture frame to give an impression of age and natural wear.

**Double Mat (Mount)** One mat (mount) laid on top of another; the upper one has a larger cut-out.

**Dry Mounting** Hot-press method of attaching a picture to a backing material by means of inserting heat-soluble film between them.

**Embossing** (1) In picture framing the process of passing molding under an engraved metal roller heated by a gas jet. The engraved pattern is produced on the molding by the combination of heat and pressure. (2) In mat (mount) decoration, the technique of scoring lines with a blunt-ended tool.

**Folien Method** Technique for applying gold-foil bead to molding.

**Foxing** Yellow-brown discoloration of art-on-paper caused by mildew.

**Gesso** Preparation made of rabbitskin glue and gilder's whiting (finely-powdered chalk) used to provide a base for finishes applied to moldings.

**Glazing Gun** Device that fires darts to fix glass, artwork, mat (mount) and backing board into rabbet (rebate) of frame.

**Graining** Abrading molding, especially of pine, to enhance the appearance of the grain.

**Heat Sealing** Hot-press bonding of a thin plastic protective film to surface of artwork.

**Insert** A frame mounted within the main frame, usually close to the edge of the picture and often gilded or fabric-covered; also called a slip.

**Intaglio** Engraved or incised figure or design cut into the surface of a hard material, such as molding.

**Japan Oil Size** Medium for binding metallic pigments used in powder gilding.

**Lacquer** A transparent coating applied to moldings to protect the surface and provide an interesting finish.

**Lining** Method of attaching an old or damaged canvas to a new support, usually another piece of canvas.

**Mast** Substance formerly used as material for making decorative finishes for molding. It has now been replaced by wood pulp.

**Mat** or **Mount** Board into which a bevel-edged aperture is cut to display an artwork or other subject. Originally its purpose was to separate the picture from the glass sheet, and this is still an important part of its function.

**Mat Cutter** Machine for cutting bevel-edged apertures in mats (mounts).

**Mirror Plate** Metal plate used for secure and permanent fixing of a framed picture to a wall or other surface.

**Miter** The beveled end of a length of molding that is to form one side of a frame. In a four-sided frame, a miter is cut at an angle of 45 degrees, each miter joint forming a right-angle.

**Mount:** *see* **Mat**

**Mount Cutter:** *see* **Mat Cutter**

**Ormolu** Pale yellow, alcohol-based lacquer used to protect a gilded surface.

**Patina** (1) Surface appearance of wood or metal beautified by age and use. (2) Type of lacquer used to emulate such an appearance.

**Quirk** The angles or folds in the molding, i.e. the points at which it changes direction and where any overlaps in paint application will be less noticeable.

**Rabbet** or **Rebate** Stepped or grooved section of a molding into which the glass, mat (mount), subject, and backing board are fitted when the frame is assembled.

**Rabbitskin Glue** Brown gelatin adhesive made from the skins and bones of animals.

**Rebate:** *see* **Rabbet**

**Running Pattern** Repeated decorative motif on a molding.

**Schlagg Leaf** Alloy of brass, copper and zinc in variable proportions, used as substitute for gold leaf; also known as Dutch, or gilt, metal leaf.

**Scumble** Thin layer of paint used to modify appearance of a darker paint beneath.

**Shooting Board** Stepped wooden block that holds a molding at an angle of 45 degrees to enable a plane to trim the miter.

**Sight Edge** The top, inner edge of the molding, which overlaps the image area, once made up into a frame.

**Size** Animal glue thinned with water.

**Slip:** *see* **Insert**

**Spoon Groove** Scooped profile on molding.

**Stretcher** Expandable wooden frame to which a canvas is attached under tension.

**Strut Back** Hinged support attached to backing board to enable a small framed picture to stand upright.

**Tacking Gun** Stapling gun used when stretching needlework and other material for framing.

**Tacking Iron** Electrically heated iron for tacking dry mount tissue in place before transferring to press.

**Tempera** Pigment traditionally bound with egg but, in framing, more usually with size.

**Vacuum Coating** Factory method of applying water-based stains to molding.

**Veneer** Thin layer or inlay of fine-quality or rare wood applied as a decorative finish to molding.

**Wash** Highly diluted, often transparent paint.

**Wash-line** Panel on a mat (mount) formed by a number of ink lines, within which is an area in a pale pastel shade.

**Wax Amalgam** Metal powder suspended in solution of waxes in mineral spirits (white spirit).

**Wet Mounting** Method of sticking a picture to a backing using a size or spray glue; also called "cold mounting".

**Whiting, Gilder's** Finely ground and sifted chalk; used to make gesso.

# DIRECTORY OF SUPPLIERS

This directory is organized into chapters, each of which is divided into the various items of equipment or materials; these in turn are subdivided into countries, with suppliers in the U.S.A., the U.K., Australia and New Zealand listed separately. The addresses and telephone and fax numbers of all suppliers listed will be found in the alphabetical section at the end of the directory.

## THE WORKSHOP

### Miter Cutters (guillotine and saw)

**UNITED STATES**
Art Materials, Frames & Moulding Co Inc
American Design & Engineering Inc
AMP International/Putnam Inc
CTD Machine Inc
Clark Moulding
Colorado Moulding Co
Framing Supply Center
Janow Wholesale Frame Inc
Larson-Juhl
M & M Distributors
Miter Master Inc
Pistorius Machine Co
Presto Frame & Moulding
Print Mount Co, Inc
Regal Frames, Inc
Roanoke Moulding Des
S & W Framing Supplies
Southern Moulding & Supply Co
United Mfrs Supplies Inc
Zinsel Company, Inc

**UNITED KINGDOM**
D & W Art Products
Falcon Art Supplies
Framers' Equipment Intl Ltd
F. W. Holroyd Ltd
Lion Picture Framing Supplies
Magnolia Mouldings (Sales) Ltd
Origin Framing Supplies
James Robinson Ltd
K. Scharf Ltd
D & J Simons & Sons Ltd
Sisslings (Mouldings) Ltd

**AUSTRALIA**
Frames Equipment Co
Gary McLean Framing Supplies
Kosnar Framing Equipment & Supplies

**NEW ZEALAND**
Art Picture Framers
Firenze Arts
Hart Graphics & Framing Systems Ltd
Jorwin Industries Ltd
Kents Framers Ltd

### Mat (Mount) Cutters

**UNITED STATES**
Art Materials, Frames & Moulding Co Inc
Dahle USA
Fletcher Terry Co
Nielsen & Bainbridge
Seal Products Inc
Zinsel Company Inc

**UNITED KINGDOM**
D & W Art Products
Falcon Art Supplies
Framers' Equipment Intl Ltd
F. W. Holroyd Ltd
Lion Picture Framing Supplies
Magnolia Mouldings (Sales) Ltd
Origin Framing Supplies
James Robinson Ltd
K. Scharf Ltd
D & J Simons & Sons Ltd
Sisslings (Moldings) Ltd

**AUSTRALIA**
Frames Equipment Co
Gary McLean Framing Supplies
Kosnar Framing Equipment & Supplies

**NEW ZEALAND**
Art Picture Framers
Firenze Arts
Hart Graphics & Framing Systems Ltd
Jorwin Industries Ltd
Kents Framers Ltd

### Compressors

**UNITED STATES**
AMP International/Putnam Inc
CTD Machine Inc
Colorado Moulding Co
Corona Co
Larson-Juhl
M & M Distributors

Northcoast Frame Supply
Pistorius Machine Co
Roanoke Moulding Des
Southern Moulding & Supply Co
Zinsel Company Inc

**UNITED KINGDOM**
D & W Art Products
Falcon Art Supplies
Framers' Equipment Intl Ltd
F. W. Holroyd Ltd
Lion Picture Framing Supplies
Magnolia Mouldings (Sales) Ltd
Origin Framing Supplies
James Robinson Ltd
K. Scharf Ltd
D & J Simons & Sons Ltd
Sisslings (Mouldings) Ltd

**AUSTRALIA**
Frames Equipment Co
Gary McLean Framing Supplies
Kosnar Framing Equipment & Supplies

**NEW ZEALAND**
Art Picture Framers
Firenze Arts
Hart Graphics & Framing Systems Ltd
Jorwin Industries Ltd
Kents Framers Ltd

### Underpinners

**UNITED STATES**
Art Materials, Frames & Moulding Co Inc
AMP International/Putnam Inc
Milton W. Bosley Co
Colorado Moulding Co
Corona Co
Robert F. De Castro, Inc
Framing Supply Center
Janow Wholesale Frame Inc
Larson-Juhl
M & M Distributors
Pistorius Machine Co
Regal Frames, Inc
Roanoke Moulding Des
S & W Framing Supplies

Southern Moulding & Supply Co
Zinsel Company, Inc

**UNITED KINGDOM**
Budget Trading Enterprises Ltd
D & W Art Products
Euro Mouldings Ltd
Falcon Art Supplies
Framers' Equipment Intl Ltd
F. W. Holroyd Ltd
Lion Picture Framing Supplies
Magnolia Mouldings (Sales) Ltd
Origin Framing Supplies
James Robinson Ltd
K. Scharf Ltd
D & J Simons & Sons Ltd
Sisslings (Mouldings) Ltd

**AUSTRALIA**
Frames Equipment Co
Gary McLean Framing Supplies
Kosnar Framing Equipment & Supplies

**NEW ZEALAND**
Art Picture Framers
Firenze Arts
Hart Graphics & Framing Systems Ltd
Jorwin Industries Ltd
Kents Framers Ltd

### Heatseal/Dry-Mounting Press Equipment

**UNITED STATES**
Art Materials, Frames & Moulding Co Inc
AMP International/Putnam Inc
Milton W. Bosley Co
Colorado Moulding Co
Corona Co
Robert F. De Castro, Inc
Framing Supply Center
Gemini Moulding
Janow Wholesale Frame Inc
Larson-Juhl
Le Winter Moulding & Supply
M & M Distributors
Pistorius Machine Co

Regal Frames, Inc
Roanoke Moulding Des
S & W Framing Supplies
Southern Moulding & Supply Co
Specialty Tapes/One Source,
    R.S.W. Inc
West Shore Distributors
Zinsel Company, Inc

UNITED KINGDOM
Ademco Ltd
D & W Art Products
Falcon Art Supplies
Framers' Equipment Intl Ltd
F. W. Holroyd Ltd
Hot Press (Heat Sealing) Ltd
Lion Picture Framing Supplies
Origin Framing Supplies
James Robinson Ltd
Sallmetall Ltd
Seal International
D & J Simons & Sons Ltd

AUSTRALIA
Frames Equipment Co
Gary McLean Framing Supplies
Kosnar Framing Equipment &
    Supplies

NEW ZEALAND
Art Picture Framers
Firenze Arts
Hart Graphics & Framing Systems
    Ltd
Jorwin Industries Ltd
Kents Framers Ltd

## Small Ancillary Equipment

Knives, saws, files, brushes, pens,
    pliers, clamps, staplers, straight
    edges, clay-modelling tools,
    burnishing tools, etc

UNITED STATES
Art Essentials of New York, Ltd
Art Materials, Frames & Moulding
    Co Ltd
Easy-Leaf Products By Madana Mfg
Fletcher Terry Co
Framing Supply Center
M. Grumbacher, Inc
Larson-Juhl
Hunt Mfg Co
M & M Distributors
United Mfrs Supplies Inc
Zinsel Company, Inc

UNITED KINGDOM
Ashworth & Thompson Ltd
Croxley Framers' Supplies
Hang-It Framing Systems Ltd
Lion Picture Framing Supplies
Origin Framing Supplies
Seal International
D & J Simons & Sons Ltd

AUSTRALIA
Frames Equipment Co
Gary McLean Framing Supplies
Kosnar Framing Equipment &
    Supplies

NEW ZEALAND
Art Picture Framers
Firenze Arts
Hart Graphics & Framing Systems
    Ltd
Jorwin Industries Ltd
Kents Framers Ltd

## Workshop Consumables

Tapes, adhesives (rabbitskin glue,
    wood glue, etc), abrasives,
    paints, papers, cleaning
    materials, pins, screws, blades,
    etc

UNITED STATES
Art Materials, Frames & Moulding
    Co Ltd
Colorado Moulding Co
Corona Co
Easy-Leaf Products by Madana Mfg
Gemini Moulding
Larson-Juhl
Le Winter Moulding & Supply
M & M Distributors
Regal Frames, Inc
Roanoke Moulding Des
S & W Framing Supplies
Seal Products Inc
Sepp Leaf Products Inc
Southern Moulding & Supply Co
United Mfrs Supplies Inc

UNITED KINGDOM
Ashworth & Thompson Ltd
Bollom
L. Cornelissen
Croxley Framers' Supplies
Framers' Equipment Intl Ltd
Hang-It Framing Systems Ltd
Lion Picture Framing Supplies
Origin Framing Supplies
Ploton Sundries
Seal International
D & J Simons & Sons Ltd
Stuart Stevenson

AUSTRALIA
Frames Equipment Co
Gary McLean Framing Supplies
Kosnar Framing Equipment &
    Supplies

NEW ZEALAND
Art Picture Framers
Firenze Arts
Hart Graphics & Framing Systems
    Ltd
Jorwin Industries Ltd
Kents Framers Ltd

# THE MAT
## (MOUNT)

### Board
UNITED STATES
Art Materials, Frames & Moulding
    Co Inc
Cardcrafts Inc
Columbia Corp, Artists' Supplies
    Div
Crescent Cardboard Co
Fomebords Co
Hunt Mfg Co
Miller Cardboard Co
Primex Plastics Corp
Savage Universal Corp
Seal Products Inc
United Mfrs Supplies Inc

UNITED KINGDOM
Arquati (UK) Ltd
Ashworth & Thompson Ltd
Atlantis Paper Co
Croxley Framer's Supplies
Daler Framing
D & J Simons & Sons Ltd
Euro Mouldings
Lawrence & Aitken
Lion Picture Framing Supplies
Magnolia Mouldings (Sales) Ltd
Masters Wilkerson Co Ltd
Meridian Mouldings Ltd
Nielsen Ltd
Origin Framing Supplies
Priory Mouldings
D & J Simons & Sons Ltd
Slater Harrison & Co Ltd
Westward Art Frames

AUSTRALIA
Aparan Holdings
Mattboard

NEW ZEALAND
Beca Fine Arts Ltd
Hart Graphics & Framing Systems
    Ltd
Kwikframe
Peter Small Ltd
Webster's

### Handheld Mat (Mount) Cutters

UNITED STATES
Art Materials, Frames & Moulding
    Co Inc
Colorado Moulding Co
Dahle USA
Robert F. De Castro, Inc
Fomebords Co
Framing Supply Center
Larson-Juhl
Le Winter Moulding & Supply
M & M Distributors

Michael Business Machines Corp
Pistorius Machine Co
Regal Frames, Inc
Roanoke Moulding Des
S & W Framing Supplies
T.C. Moulding & Supply
United Mfrs Supplies Inc
Zorba Frame & Moulding

UNITED KINGDOM
Ashworth & Thompson Ltd
D & W Art Products
Falcon Art Supplies
Framers' Equipment Intl Ltd
F. W. Holroyd Ltd
Keencut Ltd
Lion Picture Framing Supplies
Origin Framing Supplies
James Robinson Ltd
D & J Simons & Sons Ltd

AUSTRALIA
Aparan Holdings
Mattboard

NEW ZEALAND
Beca Fine Arts Ltd
Hart Graphics & Framing Systems
    Ltd
Kwikframe
Peter Small Ltd
Webster's

### Mat (Mount) Decoration Materials

Paints and powders, corner-marking
    devices, ruling pens, etc.

UNITED STATES
Art Materials, Frames & Moulding
    Co Inc
Easy-Leaf Products By Madana Mfg
M & M Distributors
Sepp Leaf Products Inc
United Mfrs Supplies Inc

UNITED KINGDOM
Ashworth & Thompson Ltd
Atlantis Paper Co
Bollom
L. Cornelissen
D & W Art Products
Falcon Art Supplies
Framers' Equipment
Lion Picture Framing Supplies
Ploton Sundries
Origin Framing Supplies
D & J Simons & Sons Ltd
Stuart Stevenson

AUSTRALIA
Aparan Holdings
Mattboard

NEW ZEALAND
Beca Fine Arts Ltd
Hart Graphics & Framing Systems
    Ltd

Kwikframe
Peter Small Ltd
Webster's

## *Decorative Papers, Wood Veneer*

UNITED STATES
AGF Inc
Art Materials, Frames & Moulding Co Inc
Colorado Moulding Co
Crescent Cardboard Co
Framing Supply Center
Gemini Moulding
Harvey Fabrics
Janow Wholesale Frame
Kansas City Moulding
Larson-Juhl
M & M Distributors
Miller Cardboard Co
Nielsen & Bainbridge
Northcoast Frame Supply
Regal Frames, Inc
Roanoke Moulding Des
S & W Framing Supplies
Southern Moulding & Supply Co
Specialty Tapes/One Source, RSW, Inc
Sprague Hathaway Co, Inc
T.C. Moulding & Supply
United Mfrs Supplies Inc
West Shore Distributors
Zinsel Company, Inc

UNITED KINGDOM
Arquati (UK) Ltd
Ashworth & Thompson Ltd
Atlantis Paper Co
D & W Art Products
Falcon Art Supplies
Framers' Equipment
Magnolia Mouldings (Sales) Ltd
Origin Framing Supplies
D & J Simons & Sons Ltd

AUSTRALIA
Aparan Holdings
Mattboard

NEW ZEALAND
Beca Fine Arts Ltd
Hart Graphics & Framing Systems Ltd
Kwikframe
Peter Small Ltd
Webster's

## THE

## — MOLDING —

## *Moldings*

Wood and aluminum; plain, carved, embossed, etc

UNITED STATES
Art Materials, Frames & Moulding Co Inc
Colorado Moulding Co
Framing Supply Center
Janow Wholesale Frame Inc
Lamarche Moulding Co
Larson-Juhl
Le Winter Moulding & Supply
M & M Distributors
Presto Frame & Moulding
Print Mount Co, Inc
Roanoke Moulding Des
S & W Framing Supplies
Southern Moulding & Supply Co
T.C. Moulding & Supply Co
United Mfrs Supplies Inc
Zinsel Company, Inc

UNITED KINGDOM
Aluminium Framing Supplies
Arquati (UK) Ltd
Ashworth & Thompson Ltd
Atlantis Paper Co
Byron Mouldings
Daler Framing
D & J Simons & Sons Ltd
D & W Art Products
Euro Mouldings Ltd
Falcon Art Supplies
Frinton Mouldings Ltd
F. W. Holroyd Ltd
Hang-It Framing Systems Ltd
Magnolia Mouldings (Sales) Ltd
Marpatt Ltd
Masters Wilkerson Co Ltd
Meridian Mouldings Ltd
Nielsen Ltd
Origin Framing Supplies
PFM (Scottish & Northern Sales) Ltd
Priory Mouldings
James Robinson Ltd
K. Scharf Ltd
D & J Simons & Sons Ltd
Sisslings (Mouldings) Ltd
Sullivans Mouldings Ltd
U.K. Mouldings Ltd
Westward Art Frames

AUSTRALIA
Harper & Sandilands Pty Ltd
Hughes Mouldings
Marks & Co Pty Ltd
Timber Detail Mouldings

NEW ZEALAND
Avon Picture Mouldings Ltd
Maple
Picture Moulding Distributing Co Ltd
Peter Small
The Willeston Gallery Ltd

## *Stains, Dyes, Varnishes*

UNITED STATES
Albums, Inc

Colorado Moulding Co
M & M Distributors
United Mfrs Supplies Inc

UNITED KINGDOM
Ashworth & Thompson Ltd
Atlantis Paper Co
Croxley Framers' Supplies
D & W Art Products
Falcon Art Supplies
F. W. Holroyd Ltd
James Robinson Ltd
Lion Picture Framing Supplies
James Robinson Ltd
D & J Simons & Sons Ltd

AUSTRALIA
Harper & Sandilands Pty Ltd
Hughes Mouldings
Marks & Co Pty Ltd
Timber Detail Mouldings

NEW ZEALAND
Avon Picture Mouldings Ltd
Maple
Picture Moulding Distributing Co Ltd
Peter Small
The Willeston Gallery Ltd

## *Slips & Fillets*

UNITED STATES
Art-O-Rama, Inc
Colorado Moulding Co
D.C. Framing Supply
Robert F. De Castro, Inc
Frame Supply of Houston, Inc
Framing Supply Center
Gemini Moulding
Janow Wholesale Frame Inc
Larson-Juhl
Le Winter Moulding & Supply Co
New England Frame Crafters
Northcoast Frame Supply
P B & H Moulding Co
Presto Frame & Moulding
Regal Frames Inc
Roanoke Moulding Des
Southern Moulding & Supply Co
Stewart Moulding & Frame Co
T.C. Moulding & Supply
United Mfrs Supplies Inc
West Shore Distributors
Wolsey
Zorba Frame & Moulding

UNITED KINGDOM
Ashworth & Thompson Ltd
D & W Art Products
Falcon Art Supplies
Origin Framing Supplies
James Robinson Ltd
D & J Simons & Sons Ltd

AUSTRALIA
Harper & Sandilands Pty Ltd
Hughes Mouldings
Marks & Co Pty Ltd
Timber Detail Mouldings

NEW ZEALAND
Avon Picture Mouldings Ltd
Maple
Picture Moulding Distributing Co Ltd
Peter Small
The Willeston Gallery Ltd

## *Filling Cream & Waxes*

UNITED STATES
Art Materials, Frames & Moulding Co Inc
Aztec Moulding Co
Colorado Moulding Co
Corona Co
Framing Supply Center
Gemini Moulding
M & M Distributors
Regal Frames, Inc
Roanoke Moulding Des
S & W Framing Supplies
Southern Moulding & Supply Co
T.C. Moulding & Supply
United Mfrs Supplies Inc
Zinsel Company, Inc

UNITED KINGDOM
Ashworth & Thompson Ltd
Croxley Framers' Supplies
D & W Art Products
Falcon Art Supplies
F. W. Holroyd Ltd
Lion Picture Framing Supplies
John Myland
Origin Framing Supplies
James Robinson Ltd
D & J Simons & Sons Ltd

AUSTRALIA
Harper & Sandilands Pty Ltd
Hughes Mouldings
Marks & Co Pty Ltd
Timber Detail Mouldings

NEW ZEALAND
Avon Picture Mouldings Ltd
Maple
Picture Moulding Distributing Co Ltd
Peter Small
The Willeston Gallery Ltd

## *Gesso*

UNITED STATES
Art Essentials of New York Ltd
Easy-Leaf Products By Madana Mfg
M. Grumbacher, Inc
Sepp Leaf Products Inc
M. Swift & Sons Inc
United Mfrs Supplies Inc

UNITED KINGDOM
Bollom
L. Cornelissen
Ploton Sundries
D & J Simons & Sons Ltd
Stuart Stevenson

AUSTRALIA
Harper & Sandilands Pty Ltd
Hughes Mouldings
Marks & Co Pty Ltd
Timber Detail Mouldings

NEW ZEALAND
Avon Picture Mouldings Ltd
Maple
Picture Moulding Distributing Co
 Ltd
Peter Small
The Willeston Gallery Ltd

## Gilding Materials

UNITED STATES
Art Essentials of New York Ltd
Easy-Leaf Products By Madana Mfg
Gold Leaf & Metallic Powders
S & W Framing Supplies
Sepp Leaf Products Inc
M. Swift & Sons Inc
United Mfrs Supplies Inc
United States Bronze Powders, Inc

UNITED KINGDOM
Bollom
L. Cornelissen
Ploton Sundries
D & J Simons & Sons Ltd
Stuart Stevenson

AUSTRALIA
Harper & Sandilands Pty Ltd
Hughes Mouldings
Marks & Co Pty Ltd
Timber Detail Mouldings

NEW ZEALAND
Avon Picture Mouldings Ltd
Maple
Picture Moulding Distributing Co
 Ltd
Peter Small
The Willeston Gallery Ltd

## — THE GLASS —

## Glass

Reflective and non-reflective

UNITED STATES
Art Materials, Frames & Moulding
 Inc
Aluminum Frame & Extrusion Corp
Aztec Moulding Co
Colorado Moulding Co
Robert F. De Castro, Inc
Frame Supply of Houston
Framing Supply Center
Gemini Moulding
Janow Wholesale Frame Inc
Larson-Juhl
Le Winter Moulding & Supply
M & M Distributors
Northcoast Frame Supply
Regal Frames, Inc
Roanoke Moulding Des
Sandel Glass Co

Southern Moulding & Supply Co
Sprague Hathaway Co, Inc
Sterling Mirror Co
T.C. Moulding & Supply
True Vue
United Mfrs Supplies Inc
West Shore Distributors
Zinsel Company, Inc
Zorba Frame & Moulding

UNITED KINGDOM
Concorde Glass Ltd
Glass & Mirror
K.C. Glass
Origin Framing Supplies
Priory Mouldings
Sydenham Glass Supplies Ltd
Westward Art Frames
Witting Bros Ltd

AUSTRALIA
Kenbrook Glass & Cladding Pty Ltd
Scan Pacific

NEW ZEALAND
The Glass Shoppe Ltd
Pictures & Frames

## Glass-cutting Equipment

UNITED STATES
Art Materials, Frames & Moulding
 Co Inc
Colorado Moulding Co
Robert F. De Castro, Inc
Fletcher Terry Co
Framing Supply Center
Gemini Moulding
H. F. Esterly Co
Larson-Juhl
Le Winter Moulding & Supply
M & M Distributors
Northcoast Framing Supplies
Regal Frames, Inc
Roanoke Moulding Des
S & W Framing Supplies
Southern Moulding & Supply Co
T.C. Moulding & Supply
Sterling Mirror Co
West Shore Distributors
United Mfrs Supplies Inc
Zinsel Co, Inc

UNITED KINGDOM
Ashworth & Thompson Ltd
Croxley Framers' Supplies
D & W Art Products
Falcon Art Suppliers
F. W. Holroyd Ltd
Hang-It Framing Systems Ltd
Lion Picture Framing Supplies
Origin Framing Supplies
James Robinson Ltd
D & J Simons & Sons Ltd
Westward Art Frames

AUSTRALIA
Kenbrook Glass & Cladding Pty Ltd
Scan Pacific

NEW ZEALAND
The Glass Shoppe Ltd
Pictures & Frames

## — THE FRAME —

## Backing Board

UNITED STATES
Art Materials, Frames & Moulding
 Co Inc
Cardcrafts Inc
Crescent Cardboard Co
Fomebords
Hunt Mfg Co, Bienfang
M & M Distributors
Miller Cardboard Co
Primex Plastics Corp
Savage Universal Corp
Seal Products Inc
United Mfrs Supplies Inc

UNITED KINGDOM
Ademco Ltd
Arquati (UK) Ltd
Ashworth & Thompson Ltd
Atlantis Paper Co
Daler Framing
Euro Mouldings
Falcon Art Supplies
Hang-It Framing Systems Ltd
F. W. Holroyd Ltd
Lion Picture Framing Supplies
Magnolia Mouldings (Sales) Ltd
Masters Wilkerson Co Ltd
Meridian Mouldings Ltd
Nielsen Ltd
Origin Framing Supplies
Priory Mouldings
James Robinson Ltd
K. Scharf Ltd
D & J Simons & Sons Ltd
Sisslings (Mouldings) Ltd
U.K. Mouldings Ltd
Westward Art Frames

AUSTRALIA
Art Barnes of Australia
Frames Equipment Co
Geometrics Contemporary Art

NEW ZEALAND
A1 Print Service
Camellia International Ltd
The Frame Workshop
Panorama Enterprises

## Canvas Stretchers

UNITED STATES
Art Materials, Frames & Moulding
 Co Inc
Colorado Moulding Co
Corona Co
Robert F. De Castro, Inc
Frame & Art Depot
Gemini Moulding
Larson-Juhl

M & M Distributors
Regal Frames, Inc
S & W Framing Supplies
T.C. Moulding & Supply
United Mfrs Supplies Inc
Wolsey
Zorba Frame & Moulding

UNITED KINGDOM
Ashworth & Thompson Ltd
Euro Mouldings
Falcon Art Supplies
Framers' Corner
Lion Picture Framing Supplies
Origin Framing Supplies
Priory Mouldings
Magnolia Mouldings (Sales) Ltd
D & J Simons & Sons Ltd
Sisslings (Mouldings) Ltd
Westward Art Frames

AUSTRALIA
Art Barnes of Australia
Frames Equipment Co
Geometrics Contemporary Art

NEW ZEALAND
A1 Print Service
Camellia International Ltd
The Frame Workshop
Panorama Enterprises

## Protective Coatings

UNITED STATES
Albums, Inc
Easy-Leaf Products By Madana Mfg
M & M Distributors
S & W Framing Supplies
United Mfrs Supplies Inc

UNITED KINGDOM
Ashworth & Thompson Ltd
Atlantis Paper Co
D & J Simons & Sons Ltd
Falcon Art Supplies
Lion Picture Framing Supplies
Origin Framing Supplies
Westward Art Frames

AUSTRALIA
Art Barnes of Australia
Frames Equipment Co
Geometrics Contemporary Art

NEW ZEALAND
A1 Print Service
Camellia International Ltd
The Frame Workshop
Panorama Enterprises

## HANGING EQUIPMENT

Wires and cords, rings and eyes,
 wall hooks, back fixings, hanging
 plates, picture lights, bows,

rosettes, special hooks and
hanging devices, etc

### UNITED STATES
Art Materials, Frames & Moulding
  Co Inc
Art Material Service, Inc
Colorado Moulding Co
Robert F. De Castro, Inc
Frame Supply of Houston, Inc
Frameware Inc
Framing Supply Center
Gemini Moulding
Janow Wholesale Frame Inc
Larson-Juhl
Le Winter Moulding & Supply
M & M Distributors
Moore Push Pin Co
Northcoast Frame Supply
Regal Frames, Inc
S & W Framing Supplies
Southern Moulding & Supply Co
T.C. Moulding & Supply
United Mfrs Supplies Inc
West Shore Distributors
Zinsel Company, Inc
Zorba Frame & Moulding

### UNITED KINGDOM
Atlantis Paper Co
Ashworth & Thompson Ltd
Croxley Framers' Supplies
D & W Art Products
Falcon Art Supplies
Hang-It Framing Systems Ltd
F. W. Holroyd Ltd
Lion Picture Framing Supplies
Magnolia Mouldings (Sales) Ltd
Meridian Mouldings Ltd
Origin Framing Supplies
Priory Mouldings
James Robinson Ltd
K. Scharf Ltd
D & J Simons & Sons Ltd
Sisslings (Mouldings) Ltd
Westward Art Frames

### AUSTRALIA
Amsta Art Materials & Stationery
  Pty Ltd
Aparan Holdings
Kosnar Framing Equipment &
  Supplies

### NEW ZEALAND
Art Picture Framers
Eastern Picture Framing Ltd
Focus Frame Centre
KS Thompson

# CONSERVATION

## Conservation Products

### UNITED STATES
Acid-free boards, papers, foam
  cores, tapes, etc

### UNITED STATES
Art Materials, Frames & Moulding
  Co Inc
Aluminum Frame & Extrusion Corp
Aztec Moulding Co
Colorado Moulding Co
Columbia Corp (Artists' Supplies
  Div)
Crescent Cardboard Co
D.C. Framing Supply
Robert F. De Castro, Inc
Fomebords Co
Frame Supply of Houston, Inc
Framing Supply Center
Gemini Moulding
Hunt Mfg Co, Bienfang
Janow Wholesale Frame Inc
Larson-Juhl
Le Winter Moulding & Supply
M & M Distributors
Miller Cardboard Co
Northcoast Frame Supply
Primex Plastics Corp

Regal Frames, Inc
Roanoke Moulding Des
S & W Framing Supplies
Savage Universal Corp
Southern Moulding & Supply Co
Specialty Tapes/One Source,
  R.S.W, Inc
T.C. Moulding & Supply
United Mfrs Supplies Inc
West Shore Distributors
Zinsel Company, Inc
Zorba Frame & Moulding

### UNITED KINGDOM
Ashworth & Thompson Ltd
Atlantis Paper Co
Croxley Framers' Supplies
Daler Framing
Falcon Art Supplies
Lion Picture Framing Supplies
Nielsen Ltd
Origin Framing Supplies
D & J Simons & Sons Ltd
Westward Art Frames

### AUSTRALIA
Lennox Gallery
Messis Picture Gallery Pty Ltd

### NEW ZEALAND
Downtown Hilton Gallery
Focus Frame Centre

# — PACKAGING —

## Display and Packaging Products

### UNITED STATES
Art Materials, Frames & Moulding
  Co Inc
Colorado Moulding Co
Gemini Moulding

Hobby Hill
House of Troy
Janow Wholesale Frame Inc
Larson-Juhl
M & M Distributors
Northcoast Frame Supply
S & W Framing Supplies
Southern Moulding & Supply Co
T.C. Moulding & Supply Co
United Mfrs Supplies Inc
Walker Systems Inc
West Shore Distributors
Zinsel Co, Inc

### UNITED KINGDOM
Ashworth & Thompson Ltd
Croxley Framers' Supplies
D & W Art Products
Falcon Art Supplies
Hang-It Framing Systems Ltd
F. W. Holroyd Ltd
Lion Picture Framing Supplies
Origin Framing Supplies
Postal Products Ltd
James Robinson Ltd
D & J Simons & Sons Ltd
Westward Art Frames

### AUSTRALIA
Amsta Art Materials & Stationery
  Pty Ltd
Frames Equipment Co

### NEW ZEALAND
Art Barn
Framers Supply Depot

# — ALPHABETICAL LIST OF SUPPLIERS —

Key: T = Telephone number
F = Fax number

A1 Print Service 158 Vivian Street,
  Wellington, New Zealand / T: (04)
  848 422
Ademco Ltd 12–13 Blenheim Road,
  Cressex Industrial Estate, High
  Wycombe, Bucks HP12 3RS, U.K. /
  T: 0494 448661 / F: 0494 28730
AGF Inc 11551 Adie Road, Maryland
  Heights, MO 63043, U.S.A. / T:
  (314) 991–3311, (800) 332–2467
Albums, Inc, P.O. Box 81757,
  Cleveland, OH 44181, U.S.A. / T:
  (216) 243–2127, (800) 662–1000

Aluminum Frame & Extrusion Corp 18
  Commerce Road, Fairfield, NJ
  07004, U.S.A. / T: (201) 575 4814,
  (800) 524 0583 / F: (201) 575 1559
Aluminium Framing Supplies 40–44
  Peel Road, London E18 2LG, U.K. /
  T: 081 505 3434 / F: 081 506 1879
American Design & Engineering Inc
  4543 Woodland Drive, Woodbury,
  MN 55125, U.S.A. / T: (612) 459–
  7400, (800) 441–1388
AMP International/Putnam Inc 24289
  Indoplex Circle, Farmington Hills,
  MI 48018, U.S.A. / T: (313) 477–
  1700, (800) 322–4204 / F: (313)
  477–5995

Amsta Art Materials & Stationery Pty
  Ltd 14/50–52 Malvery Street,
  Bayswater, Vic. 3153, Australia / T:
  03 720 2000 / F: 03 720 2665
Aparan Holdings 882 Canterbury
  Road, Lakemba, NSW 2195,
  Australia / T: 02 750 8800 / F: 02
  750 8177
Arquati (UK) Ltd 2 Wolseley Road,
  Kempston, Beds, MK42 7AY, U.K. /
  T: 0234 857488 / F: 0234 840190
Art Barn 153 Broadway, New Market,
  New Zealand / T: (09) 520 5452
Art Barnes of Australia 192 Newell
  Street, Westcourt, Cairns, Qld 4870,
  Australia / T: 070 54 6555 / F: 070
  54 7076

Art Essentials of New York Ltd Three Cross Road, Suffern, NY 10901, U.S.A. / T: (913) 368–1100

Art Material Service, Inc 700 Joyce Kilmer Avenue, New Brunswick, NJ 08901, U.S.A. / T: (201) 545–8888, / F: (201) 545–9166

Art Materials, Frames & Moulding Co Inc P.O. Box 5265, 1205 Putman Drive, N.W., Huntsville, AL 35816, U.S.A. / T: (205) 837–9710, (800) 572–2028 / F: (205) 837–0712

Art-O-Rama, Inc P.O. Box 829, 510 Fifth Avenue, Pelham, NY 10803, U.S.A. / T: (914) 738–1138, (800) 421–2438 / F: (914) 738–1871

Art Picture Framers 502 Mt Eden Road, Mt Eden, New Zealand / T: (09) 688 961

Ashworth & Thompson Ltd Freeston Drive, Blenheim Industrial Estate, Bulwell, Notts NG6 8HJ, U.K. / T: 0602 278504 / F: 0602 770152

Atlantis Paper Co Gulliver's Wharf, 105 Wapping Lane, London E1 9RW, U.K. / T: 071 481 3784 / F: 071 480 5811

Avon Picture Mouldings Ltd 142 Carlyle Street, Sydenham, Christchurch, New Zealand / T & F: (03) 667 060

Aztec Moulding Co 3835 Noreth Oracle Road, Tucson, AZ 85705, U.S.A. / T: (602) 293–1752, (800) 234–4421 / F: (602) 293–0442

Beca Fine Arts Ltd 43 Cleveland Street, Brooklyn, New Zealand / T: (04) 850 724

Bollom 15 Theobalds Road, London WC1, U.K. / T: 071 242 0313

Milton W. Bosley Co 151 8th Avenue N.W., Glen Burnie, MD 21061, U.S.A. / T: (301) 761–7727, (800) 638–5010 / F: (301) 553–0575

Budget Trading Enterprises Ltd 57–9 Station Road, Harrow, Middlesex, U.K. / T: 081 863 7614

Byron Mouldings Ashley Industrial Estate East, Bradley Junction, Leeds Road, Huddersfield HD2 1UR, U.K. / T: 0484 434874 / F: 0484 519552

Camellia International 24 Allright Place, Mt Wellington, New Zealand / T: (09) 570 1216

Cardcrafts Inc 44–01 21st Street, Long Island City, NY 11101, U.S.A. / T: (718) 392–8888, (800) 777–MATS

Clark Moulding 11587 Hillguard Road, Dallas, TX 75243, U.S.A. / T: (214) 340–5097, (800) 527–7082 / F: (214) 341–4164

Colorado Moulding Co 2606 South Raritan Circle, Englewood, CO 80110, U.S.A. / T: (303) 922–1919, (800) 322–9013 / F: (303) 934–2228

Columbia Corp, Artists' Supplies Div RTE. 295, Chatham, NY 12037, U.S.A. / T: (518) 392–4000, (800) 833–1804 / F: (518) 392–4030

Concorde Glass Ltd Concorde House, Caxton Street North, London E16 1JL, U.K. / T: 071 473 2791 / F: 071 473 2619

L. Cornelissen 105 Great Russell Street, London WC1B 3RY, U.K. / T: 071 636 1045

Corona Co 1110 E. Pike, Seattle, WA 98122, U.S.A. / T: (206) 324–7050, (800) 992–6766 / F: (206) 364–1376

Crescent Cardboard Co Box XD, 100 West Willow Road, Wheeling, IL 60090, U.S.A. / T: (708) 537–3400, (800) 323–1055

Croxley Framers' Supplies 3 Penn Place, Rickmansworth, Herts WD3 1RE, U.K. / T: 0923 778189 / F: 0923 896419

CTD Machine Inc 2300 East 11th Street, Los Angeles, CA 90021, U.S.A. / T: (213) 689–4455 / F: (213) 689–1255

D & W Art Products Edwin Avenue, Hoo Farm Industrial Estate, Kidderminster, Worcs DY11 7RA, U.K. / T: 0562 747355 / F: 0562 67891

D.C. Framing Supply 2443 South Curry Street, Carson City, NV 89703, U.S.A. / T: (702) 882–8511, (702) 882–6445

Dahle USA 6 Benson Road, Oxford, CT 06483, U.S.A. / T: (203) 264–0505, (800) 243–8145 / F: (203) 264–3714

Daler Framing Peacock Lane, Bracknell, Berks RG12 4ST, U.K. / T: 0344 862055 / F: 0344 486511

Robert F. De Castro Inc P.O. Box 51251, New Orleans, LA 70151, U.S.A. / T: (504) 891–5889, (800) 535–6886 / F: (504) 891–5907

Downtown Hilton Gallery The Walkway, Downtown Shopping Centre, Auckland, New Zealand / T: (09) 303 3836

Eastern Picture Framing Ltd Cnr Kohlmarama Road and Allurn Street, Kohlmarama, New Zealand / T: (09) 567 398

Easy-Leaf Products by Madana Mfg 947 North Cole Avenue, Los Angeles, CA 90038, U.S.A. / T: (213) 469–0856 / F: (213) 469–0940

H. F. Esterly Co RR 3, Box 890, U.S. Route 1, Wiscasset, ME 04578, U.S.A. / T: (207) 882–7017, (800) 882–7017 / F: (207) 882–7017

Euro Mouldings Ltd Decoy Road, Worthing, Sussex BN14 8JH, U.K. / T: 0903 205825 / F: 0903 206666

Falcon Art Supplies Leeds: Ridge Mills, Meanwood Road, U.K. / T: 0532 274093. Manchester: Unit 7, Sedgeley Park, George Street, Prestwich / T: 061 773 8830

Firenze Arts 1017A Dominion Road, Mt Roskill, New Zealand / T: (09) 693 463

Fletcher Terry Co 65 Spring Lane, Farmington, CT 06032, U.S.A. / T: (203) 677–7331, (800) 843–3826 / F: (203) 676–8858

Focus Frame Centre 716 Dominion Road, Balmoral, New Zealand / T: (09) 604 428

Fomebords Co 2211 North Elston Avenue, Chicago, IL 60614, U.S.A. / T: (312) 278–9200, (800) 362–6267 / F: (312) 278–9466

Frame & Art Depot 6479F Peachtree Ind. Blvd, Atlanta, GA 30360, U.S.A. / T: (404) 457–7131 / F: (404) 457–0401

Frame Supply of Houston, Inc 9630 Clarewood D-6, Houston, TX 77036, U.S.A. / T: (713) 270–0241, (800) 833–5929 / F: (713) 270–5950

The Frame Workshop 128 Ponsonby Road, Ponsonby, New Zealand / T: (09) 789 100

Framers' Corner 1–3 Rowan Street, Fosse Road North, Leicester LE3 9GP, U.K. / T: 0533 511550

Framers' Equipment Intl Ltd Unit 3, Well Lane, Danbury, Essex CM3

4AD, U.K. / T: 0245 415904 / F: 0245 416505

Framers Supply Depot 149 Stoddard Road, Mt Roskill, New Zealand / T: (09) 695 476

Frames Equipment Co 50 Rooks Road, Nunawading, Vic. 3131, Australia / T: 03 872 3600 / F: 03 872 3564

Frameware Inc 700 Route 46 West, Clifton, NJ 07013, U.S.A. / T: (201) 772–0101 / F: (201) 772–3508

Framing Supply Center 210 Burgess Road, Greensboro, NC 27410, U.S.A. / T: (919) 668–9500, (800) 638–9501 / F: (919) 668–2077

Frinton Mouldings Ltd 145 Connaught Avenue, Frinton-on-Sea, Essex CO3 9AH, U.K. / T: 0255 677040 / F: 0255 677307

Gary McLean Framing Supplies 34–36 Canterbury Road, Heathmont, Vic. 3135, Australia / T: 03 720 6405 / F: 03 729 6085

Gemini Moulding 601 South Vermont, Palatine, IL 60067, U.S.A. / T: (708) 359–2005, (800) 942–5131(IL) / F: (708) 359–2887

Geometrics Contemporary Art Unit 10, Harcourt Estate, 809–821 Botany Road, Rosebery, NSW 2018, Australia / T: 02 669 3899 / F: 02 669 1906

Glass & Mirror Unit 2, Brook Way, Leatherhead, Surrey KT22 7NA, U.K. / T: 0372 377738 / F: 0372 386315

The Glass Shoppe Ltd 506 High Street, Lower Hutt, New Zealand / T: (04) 691 094

Gold Leaf & Metallic Powders 2 Barclay Street, New York, NY10007, U.S.A. / T: (212) 267–4900, (800) 322–0323 / F: (212) 608–4245

M. Grumbacher, Inc 30 Engelhard Drive, Cranbury, NJ 08512, U.S.A. / T: (609) 655–8282, (800) 346–3278 / F: (609) 655–9114

Hang-It Framing Systems Ltd 225 Greenwich High Road, London SE10 4EG, U.K. / T: 081 858 2312 / F: 081 853 2133

Harper & Sandilands Pty Ltd 9 Almeida Crescent, South Yarra, Vic.

3141, Australia / T: 03 826 3611 / F: 03 826 2846

Hart Graphics & Framing Systems Ltd 37 Selwyn Street, Onehunga, Auckland, New Zealand / T: (09) 643 516 / F: (09) 644 536

Harvey Fabrics P.O. Box 668, Oyster Bay, NY 11771, U.S.A. / T: (516) 922–9180, (800) 221–1096

Hobby Hill 2321 North Keystone Avenue, Chicago, IL 60639, U.S.A. / T: (312) 342–5700 / F: (312) 342–5705

F. W. Holroyd Ltd 9–11 George Street, Glasgow G1 1PY, U.K. / T: 041 552 2024

Hot Press (Heat Sealing) Ltd Unit 4–5, Burbidge Road, Bordesley Green, Birmingham B9 4US, U.K. / T: 021 771 2529 / F: 021 771 2540

House of Troy Silver Ridge Road, Hyde Park, VT 05655, U.S.A. / T: (802) 888–7984, (800) 428–5367 / F: (802) 888–2942

Hughes Mouldings 37 Unwin Street, Moorooka, Qld 4195, Australia / T: 07 848 0126 / F: 07 892 3424

Hunt Mfg Co, Bienfang 230 South Broad Street, Philadelphia, PA 19102, U.S.A. / T: (215) 732–7700

Janow Wholesale Frame Inc 17 Andover Drive, West Hartford, CT 06110, U.S.A. / T: (203) 953–9662, (800) 225–6705(CT) / F: (203) 953–8044

Jorwin Industries Ltd 138 Captain Springs Road, Te Papapa, Auckland, New Zealand / T: (09) 664 995

K.C. Glass Unit 23, Central Industrial Estate, Cable Street, Wolverhampton WV2 2RJ, U.K. / T: 0902 458882 / F: 0902 456417

Kansas City Moulding 9343 West 74th Street, Shawnee Mission, KS 66204, U.S.A. / T: (913) 432–3800, (800) 255–0147 / F: (913) 262–0994

Keencut Ltd Tyson Courtyard, Weldon South Industrial Estate, Corby, Northants NN18 8AZ, U.K. / T: 0536 63158 / F: 0536 204227

Kenbrock Glass & Cladding Pty Ltd 3/2 Aquatic Drive, Frenchs Forest, NSW 2086, Australia / T: 02 451 1600 / F: 02 451 6082

Kents Framers Ltd 170 Parnell Road, Parnell, New Zealand / T: (09) 393 821 / F: (09) 393 822

Kosnar Framing Equipment & Supplies 550 Mt Alexander Road, Ascot Vale, Vic. 3032, Australia / T: 03 370 5044 / F: 03 370 8882

Kwikframe 4132 The Concourse, Henderson, New Zealand / T & F: (09) 837 2606

Lamarche Moulding Co 20780 Leapwood Avenue, Carson, CA 90746, U.S.A. / T: (213) 515–0011, (800) 423–0092(CA) / F: (213) 515–0475

Larson-Juhl California: 9825 Pioneer Blvd, Santa Fe Springs, CA 90670, U.S.A. / T: (213) 942–2330, (800) 624–7034(CA) / F: (213) 949–1328. Colorado: 6385 West 52nd Avenue, Arvada, CO 80002 / T: (303) 420–3123, (800) 826–9848(CO) / F: (303) 420–2609. Florida: 4330 South Frontage Road, Lakeland, FL 33801 / T: (813) 688–3671, (800) 627–1410 / F: (813) 682–1449. Georgia: 4320 International Blvd, Norcross, GA 30093 / T: (404) 564–3012, (800) 822–2195(GA) / F: (404) 925–4176. Illinois: 775 Mittle Drive, Wood Dale, IL 60191 / T: (312) 595–2232, (800) 323–8891(IL) / F: (312) 595–8078. Minnesota: 7585 Equitable Drive, Eden Prairie, MN 55344 / T: (612) 937–3200, (800) 627–1400 / F: (612) 937–3251. Ohio: 6780 Miller Road, Brecksville, OH 44141 / T: (216) 526–4680, (800) 627–5591 / F: (216) 526–2130. Pennsylvania: 427 Sargon Way, Horsham, PA 19044 / T: (215) 674–0138, (800) 426–5811 / F: (215) 674–4895. Texas: 14034 Welch Road, Farmers Branch, TX 75244 / T: (214) 458–9898, (800) 442–1371(TX) / F: (214) 991–0594. Washington: 6020 6th Avenue South, Seattle, WA 98106 / T: (206) 767–0622, (800) 627–1500 / F: (206) 762–1206. Wisconsin: 422 Third Street West, Ashland, WI 54806 / T: (715) 682–5257, (800) 472–7363(WI) / F: (715) 682–5583

Lawrence & Aitken Albion Works,

Kimberley Road, London NW6 7SL, U.K. / T: 071 624 8135 / F: 071 328 0760

Le Winter Moulding & Supply 137 23rd Street, Pittsburgh, PA 15215, U.S.A. / T: (412) 782–2220, (800) 633–7776 / F: (412) 782–1192

Lennox Gallery 1 Palmer Street, Parramatta, NSW 2150, Australia / T: 02 630 6533

Lion Picture Framing Supplies 148 Garrison Street, Bordesley, Birmingham B9 4BN, U.K. / T: 021 773 1230 / F: 021 771 2540

M & M Distributors Box 96, Tennant, NJ 07763, U.S.A. / T: (201) 780–7747, (800) 526–2302 / F: (201) 431–3732

Magnolia Mouldings (Sales) Ltd Magnolia House, Rutherford Drive, Park Farm South, Wellingborough, Northants NN8 3JF, U.K. / T: 0933 400500 / F: 0933 400404

Maple 190 High Street, Lower Hutt, New Zealand / T: (04) 663 820

Marks & Co Pty Ltd 20–22 Commercial Street, Marleston, SA 5033, Australia / T: 08 371 0341 / F: 08 371 1392

Marpatt Ltd 72 Abbots Road, Leicester LE5 1DB, U.K. / T: 0533 763995 / F: 0533 766890

Masters Wilkerson Co Ltd Unit 1, 118 Garratt Lane, Wandsworth, London SW18 4EG, U.K. / T: 081 870 5251 / F: 081 870 9469

Mattboard 115 Highbury Road, Burwood, Vic. 3125, Australia / T: 03 888 8225 / F: 03 888 8226

Meridian Mouldings Ltd The Old Maltings, Lombard Street, Orston, Notts NG13 9NG, U.K. / T: 0949 50585 / F: 0949 51274

Messis Picture Gallery Pty Ltd 374 Oxford Street, Bondi Junction, NSW 2022, Australia / T: 02 389 3753

Michael Business Machines Corp 3290 Ashley Phosphate Road, North Charleston, SC 29418, U.S.A. / T: (803) 552–2700, (800) 223–2508 / F: (803) 552–2974

Miller Cardboard Co 75 Wooster Street, New York, NY 10012, U.S.A. / T: (212) 226–0833, (800) 888–1662 / F: (212) 941–1815

Miter Master Inc 103A Otis Street, West Babylon, NY 11704, U.S.A. / T: (516) 491–5656, (800) 446–6622 / F: (516) 491–6740

Moore Push Pin Co 1300 East Mermaid Lane, Wyndmoor, PA 19118, U.S.A. / T: (215) 233–5700 / F: (215) 233–0660

John Myland 80 Norwood High Street, London SE27 9NW, U.K. / T: 081 670 9161

New England Frame Crafters, P.O. Box 814, King Court, Keene, NH 03431, U.S.A. / T: (603) 357–4614, (800) 325–6332

Nielsen & Bainbridge 40 Eisenhower Drive, Paramus, NJ 07652, U.S.A. / T: (201) 368–9191, (800) 342–0124

Nielsen Ltd Unit 7, Frogmore Industrial Estate, Acton Lane, London NW10 7NQ, U.K. / T: 081 961 0010 / F: 081 961 6368

Northcoast Frame Supply 2479 Russell Street, Cuyahoga Falls, OH 44221, U.S.A. / T: (216) 923–6144, (800) 283–2467 / F: (216) 923–8975

Origin Framing Supplies Ridges Yard, 107 Waddon New Road, Croydon, Surrey CRO 4JE, U.K. / T: 081 686 7462 / F: 081 681 3417

P.B. & H. Moulding Co 124 Pickard Drive East, Syracuse, NY 13211, U.S.A. / T: (315) 455–5602 / F: (315) 455–8748

PFM (Scottish & Northern Sales) Ltd Block 16, Unit 5, Clydesmill Road, Camberslang Investment Park, Glasgow G32 8RE, U.K. / T: 041 641 7740 / F: 041 641 0087

Panorama Enterprises Ltd 45A Panorama Road, Mt Wellington, New Zealand / T: (09) 591 914

Picture Moulding Distributing Co Ltd 29 Ward Street, Dunedin, New Zealand / T: (024) 477 0492

Pictures and Frames 11 Cook Street, Howick, New Zealand / T: (09) 535 9467

Pistorius Machine Co 1785 Express Drive North, Hauppauge, NY 11788, U.S.A. / T: (516) 582–6000 / F: (516) 582–6278

Ploton Sundries 273 Archway Road,

London N6 5AA, U.K. / T: 081 348 0315

Postal Products Ltd Reading: Unit 3B, Headley Park 10, Woodley, Berks RG5 4SW, U.K. / T: 0734 695400 / F: 0734 441267. Birmingham: 89 Brookvale Road, Witton, B6 7AR / T: 021 344 3646 / F: 021 344 3650

Presto Frame & Moulding 5 Diamond Avenue, Bethel, CT 06801, U.S.A. / T: (203) 744–4499, (800) 431–1622 / F: (203) 744–7406

Primex Plastics Corp P.O. Box 276, Garfield, NJ 07026, U.S.A. / T: (201) 470–8000, (800) 631–7061 / F: (201) 470–0965

Print Mount Co, Inc 204 Hartford Avenue, Providence, RI 02909, U.S.A. / T: (401) 351–5480 / F: (401) 351–5490

Priory Mouldings North House, Ravensmere, Beccles, Suffolk NR34 9BE, U.K. / T: 0502 714324

Regal Frames, Inc 16520 Cincennes Road, South Holland, IL 60473, U.S.A. / T: (312) 596–5400, (800) 323–4971 / F: (312) 596–5411

Roanoke Moulding Des P.O. Box 12586, Roanoke, VA 24026, U.S.A. / T: (703) 344–1677, (800) 336–9623 / F: (703) 345–4210

James Robinson Ltd London: 97 Lea Bridge Road, E10 7QR, U.K. / T: 081 558 9340 / F: 081 556 0943. Glasgow: Unit 7, Block 4A, Larkhall Industrial Estate, Lanark / T & F: 0698 887068. Liverpool: 80 Kempston Street, L3 8HL / T & F: 051 207 3834. Bristol: Unit 5, Foundry Yard, Deep Pit Road, Fishponds Trading Estate / T & F: 0272 584055

S & W Framing Supplies 120 Broadway, Garden City Park, NY 11040, U.S.A. / T: (516) 746–1000, (800) 645–3399 / F: (516) 746–6877

Sallmetall Ltd 132 Druid Street, London SE1 2HH, U.K. / T: 071 231 5429

Sandel Glass Co P.O. Box G, Springhill, KS 66083, U.S.A. / T: (800) 255–3078 / F: (913) 686–2255

Savage Universal Corp New York: 144 East 39th Street, NY 10016, U.S.A.

/ T: (212) 986–5752 / F: (212) 983–1871. Arizona: 800 West Fairmont Drive, Tempe, AZ 85282 / T: (602) 967–5882, (800) 624–8891 / F: (602) 968–1407

Scan Pacific 6 Bennett Street, Mortlake, NSW 2137, Australia / T: 02 736 1311 / F: 02 736 3245

K. Scharf Ltd Britannia Road, Waltham Cross, Herts EN8 7NY, U.K. / T: 0992 768658 / F: 0992 701287

Seal Products Inc 550 Spring Street, Naugatuck, CT 06770, U.S.A. / T: (203) 729–5201 / F: 729–5639

Sepp Leaf Products Inc 381 Park Avenue South, Suite 1312, New York, NY 10016, U.S.A. / T: (212) 683–2840

D & J Simons & Sons Ltd 122–150 Hackney Road, London E2 7QL, U.K. / T: 071 739 3744 / F: 071 739 4452

Sisslings (Mouldings) Ltd Merrydale Road, Euroway Estate, Bradford, West Yorks BD4 6SD, U.K. / T: 0274 685353 / F: 0274 651363

Slater Harrison & Co Ltd Lower House Mills, Bollington, Macclesfield SK10 5HW, U.K. / T: 0625 573155 / F: 0625 572792

Peter Small Ltd Auckland: 29 Beach Road, New Zealand / T: (09) 732 584 / F: (09) 732 583. Christchurch: 190 St Asaph Street / T: (03) 664 464 / F: (03) 654 814

Southern Moulding & Supply Co 129 Armour Drive N.E., Atlanta, GA 30324, U.S.A. / T: (404) 872–0775, (800) 241–5499 / F: (404) 872–0920

Specialty Tapes/One Source, R.S.W. Inc 1405 16th Street, Racine, WI 53403, U.S.A. / T: (414) 634–6688, (800) 545–8273 / F: (414) 634–4293

Sprague Hathaway Co, Inc 171B Merrimac Street, North Woburn, MA 01801, U.S.A. / T: (617) 935–6065, (800) 462–5230(MA) / F: (617) 938–0432

Sterling Mirror Co 6700 Distribution Drive, Beltsville, MD 20705, U.S.A. / T: (301) 937–0333, (800) 888–WINK / F: (301) 595–4104

Stuart Stevenson 68 Clerkenwell Road,

London EC1M 5QA, U.K. / T: 071 253 1691

Stewart Moulding & Frame Co 11500 Rojas Drive, El Paso, TX 79936, U.S.A. / T: (915) 595–1898, (800) 592–8404 / F: (915) 593–3263

Sullivans Mouldings Ltd Unit 1, Acorn Trading Estate, Gumley Road, West Thurrock, Essex RM16 1EP, U.K. / T: 0375 380432 / F: 0375 390420

M. Swift & Sons Inc P.O. Box 150, 10 Love Lane, Hartford, CT 06141, U.S.A. / T: (913) 368–1100

Sydenham Glass Supplies Ltd 107 Albert Road, London SE25 4JW, U.K. / T: 081 654 7535 / F: 081 654 3669

T.C. Moulding & Supply 1901 Oakcrest Avenue, St Paul, MN 55113, U.S.A. / T: (612) 636–6646, (800) 735–3025 / F: (612) 636–8153

KS Thompson 148 Great South Road, Remuera, New Zealand / T: (09) 520 0578

Timber Detail Mouldings 16–18 Sammut Street, Smithfield, NSW 2164, Australia / T: 02 604 6900 / F: 02 725 3357

True Vue 1315 N. North Branch, Chicago, IL 60022, U.S.A. / T: (312) 943–4200, (800) 621–8339 / F: (312) 943–2938

U.K. Mouldings Ltd Framers House, Lanrick Road, London E14 0JF, U.K. / T: 081 987 5206

United Mfrs Supplies Inc 80 Gordon Drive, Syosset, NY 11791, U.S.A. / T: (516) 433–8980, (800) 645–7260 / F: (516) 496–7968

United States Bronze Powders, Inc P.O. Box 31, Flemington, NJ 08822, U.S.A. / T: (201) 782–5454 / F: (201) 782–3489

Walker Systems Inc 250 South Lake Avenue, Duluth, MN 55802, U.S.A. / T: (218) 722–5945 / F: (218) 722–5053

Webster's 44 Manners Street, Wellington City, New Zealand / T: (04) 854 136

West Shore Distributors 871 Canterbury Road, Unit 1, Westlake, OH 44145, U.S.A. / T: (216) 835–5600, (800) 344–8141 / F: (216) 835–8654

Westward Art Frames Cornwall: Duchy, Kelly Bray, Callington, PL7 8EX, U.K. / T: 0579 83523 / F: 0579 84043. Manchester: Moston Road, Middleton, Lancs M24 1SE / T: 061 655 3990 / F: 061 655 3949

The Willeston Gallery 342 Lambton Quay, Wellington, New Zealand / T: (04) 730 664

Witting Bros Ltd The Teardrop Centre, London Road, Swanley, Kent BR8 8TS, U.K. / T: 0322 614641 / F: 0322 615139

Wolsey P.O. Box 486, 15110 East Nelson, City of Industry, CA 91747, U.S.A. / T: (818) 336–4575, (800) 426–1057(CA) / F: (818) 333–5154

Zinsel Company, Inc 712 L & A Road, Metairie, LA 70001, U.S.A. / T: (504) 834–7240, (800) 452–7211(LA) / F: (504) 834–7255

Zorba Frame & Moulding 29 Marne Street, Hamden CT 06514, U.S.A. / T: (203) 281–1111, (800) USCHOPS

## INSTITUTES

UNITED STATES: Professional Picture Framers Association, 4305 Sarellen Road, PO Box 7655, Richmond, VA 23231 / T: (804) 226 0430

UNITED KINGDOM: The Institute of British Picture Framers, 5 Elm Close, Amersham, Bucks HP6 5DD

The Fine Art Trade Guild, 16–18 Empress Place, London SW6 1TT / T: 071 381 6616 / F: 071 381 2596

AUSTRALIA: The Australian Picture Framers Association Ltd, c/o The President, 19 Glenferrie Avenue, Cremorne NSW 2090

# INDEX

## ACKNOWLEDGMENTS

The author and publisher would like to thank the following for their help in the production of the book:

Glass & Mirror for information on glass types; Lion Picture Framing Supplies for supplying the equipment for photography; Don Pierce for providing the photographs in the conservation and restoration chapter, and Rochford Mouldings for providing molding samples for photography.